BASIC ACOL

COLLINS
WINNING BRIDGE

BASIC
ACOL

BEN COHEN &
RHODA LEDERER

CollinsWillow
An Imprint of HarperCollins*Publishers*

First published in 1962 by George Allen & Unwin Ltd
Second edition 1968
Reprinted seven times
Third edition published in 1979 by Unwin® Paperbacks
Fourth edition 1981
Reprinted 1982, 1984 (twice)
Fifth edition 1984
Reprinted 1985, 1986, 1987, 1988, 1989, 1990

Revised edition published in 1993 by
Collins Willow
an imprint of HarperCollins*Publishers*, London
Reprinted 1993, 1994

A CIP catalogue record for this book
is available from the British Library

ISBN 0 00 218440 0

Set in Palatino
Printed by Scotprint Ltd, Musselburgh

Contents

Preface

In recent years the Acol system has increased in popularity and is being used by more and more established players, not only in this country but in the farthest corners of the globe. It is no longer regarded as the experts' system though, in fact, many experts and tournament players find it completely adequate for all their requirements. On the other hand, it is simple enough to be learned easily and used effectively at the humblest of levels.

Basic Acol contains 45 summary tables that cover the whole field of Acol bidding, even if only in outline. For a full and detailed study of the system you will, of course, want to read the main text book, *All About Acol*, also published by HarperCollins. You will find that the two books run parallel so that the rules and examples set out in the following pages are all strictly in line with the latest edition of *All About Acol*.

It is difficult to learn a complete system from summary tables only, without the help of a teacher or full text book, but for the learner particularly, a quick and handy book of reference is a 'must'. *Basic Acol* is planned to give you an easy way to revise anything you have been taught, or to provide the quick answer to any bidding problems which may crop up. This new edition includes all the most recent developments as well as setting out clearly, with examples, the fundamental principles on which the system is based.

A word of explanation about no-trump bidding may be helpful. As you will see in Table 11, standard Acol advocates the use of a variable no-trump, that is, 12-14 points not vulnerable and 15-17 points vulnerable, but different players have different views as to the strength required for this opening bid. Many, particularly tournament players, prefer to use weak throughout, that is, 12-14 points at any score, because of the undoubted pre-emptive value of this opening bid, and some diehards, even in this day and age, still insist on 16-18 points at all times. If you learn the mechanics of both weak and strong, you will be able to work out your own preference as well as being able to adapt yourself to your partner's wishes and – no less important – understand what is going on. From your own side's point of view it is a simple matter of knowing how many points you promise when you open 1NT, or how many points your partner is promising when he makes this bid. With this knowledge, it is not difficult to do the simple arithmetic to judge whether game or only part-score values are held between the two hands.

You will, of course, realise that summary tables such as these can take little account of tactical bids – the difference between bidding vulnerable or not vulnerable – or part-score bidding at rubber bridge. But none of these is an essential part of the system itself, and your good bidding judgement will soon develop to cope with these varying situations.

Above all, *Basic Acol* is quick, easy, brief and to the point. It is small enough to be slipped into a pocket or handbag, yet large enough to earn a place on your bookshelf.

This new edition bears little resemblance to the original *Basic Acol* that was published thirty years ago, but it says much for the reputation of the late Rhoda Lederer and Ben Cohen that a revision is now necessary.

TABLE 1   9

Hand Valuation

MILTON WORK COUNT	Ace = 4; king = 3; queen = 2; knave = 1.
Honour points	In no-trump bidding, 10 = ½ point if it is working with other honours. Thus there are 10 honour points in each suit and a total of 40 points in the pack.
As opener:	Count honour points and add 1 point for each card over four in any long suit (distributional points).
As responder:	With primary (i.e. 4-card) trump support for opener's suit, count honour points and add: 3 for a void; 2 for a singleton; 1 for a doubleton. Lacking 4-card support, value as you would for opener, i.e. honour points + long suit cards.
PLAYING TRICKS	A playing trick is a card which, in a declarer contract, can be expected to win a trick as compared with a defensive trick. Generally refers to the number of tricks available from a long suit. When calculating the number of playing tricks held you are entitled to assume a reasonable division of the outstanding cards (see examples in Table 30).

Don't get point-bound. Except for no-trump bidding, learn to value your hand for its playing value.

TABLE 2

Trick-taking or Bidding Requirements – Rough Guide

To make	Requirements
A light opening bid:	12-13 points (honours + distribution) in a hand which also contains an honest rebid *unless* partner has passed.
10 tricks for a major suit game:	26 points, honours + distribution, between the combined hands.
11 tricks for a minor suit game:	28-29 points, honours + distribution, between the combined hands.
9 tricks for a no-trump game:	25 honour points between two evenly-balanced hands, less if a 5-card (or longer) suit is also held + adequate stops in other suits.
12 tricks for a small slam:	In a suit contract, 31-33 points and a trump fit. In no-trumps on balanced hands, 33-34 points.
13 tricks for a grand slam:	37 or more points.

TABLE 3   11

Opening Suit Bids at the One-level

Requirements	Comments
An Acol light opener: 9-10 honour points with a 6-card suit or two 5-card suits	THE TEST OF WHETHER A HAND OF LOW POINT COUNT QUALIFIES FOR AN OPENING BID IS WHETHER OR NOT IT CONTAINS A SAFE REBID. These light openers do not replace normal opening bids but are added at the lower end of the scale. A 6-card suit is always rebiddable and provided two 5-card suits are adjacent *or* both black, the hand will also contain a sensible rebid.

Examples:

♠ A Q 10 8 5 2
♥ K 7 5
♦ J 3
♣ 8 4

10 honour points with a 6-card rebiddable suit + 2 distributional points.
A good attacking opening bid.

♠ Q J 9 7 5
♥ K Q 10 6 5
♦ K 3
♣ 8

Open 1♠, the higher-ranking of two equal and adjacent suits, as the hearts provide a sensible low-level rebid. Would also qualify if the hearts were clubs (two *black* suits), when the opening would be 1♣ with a rebid of 1♠ over 1♦ or 1♥ response.

♠ Q J 9 7 5
♥ K 3
♦ K Q 10 6 5
♣ 8

Same hand with suits exchanged and *not* suitable for an opening bid unless partner has previously passed because it contains no sensible rebid if partner responds 2♥ (spades too straggly for a rebid and 3♦ would be a new suit at the three-level which is *forcing*).

Requirements	Comments
Normal opening, 12+ up to 20 points. One 5-card or two biddable 4-card suits.	Normal opening bids should contain a 5-card suit as good as K-Q to five (rebiddable) or outside values providing a rebid. May vary upwards to about 20 points. Choice of opening will depend on distribution and quality. Higher end of range may well qualify for better than an opening at the one-level.
Examples: ♠ J 9 8 5 4 ♥ A K Q 6 3 ♦ 9 ♣ A 7	Open 1♠ (*not* 1♥),the higher-ranking of two equal and adjacent suits. Rebid in hearts over any response from partner except a direct spade raise.
♠ A K J 8 7 ♥ A 10 4 2 ♦ J 7 ♣ 7 3	A normal opening bid of 1♠ with a rebid of ♥ over any response other than a direct spade raise. If responder cannot then bid again (other than, perhaps, to give a preference bid of 2♠) it is unlikely that a better contract will be missed.
♠ A K 9 8 4 ♥ A 7 ♦ 5 ♣ Q 9 8 7 5	Open 1♣, *not* 1♠ with two black suits of equal length. This allows for a rebid of 1♠ over a red-suit response. Over an opening 1♠, if partner responds 2♦ or 2♥, the hand is not strong enough for a three-level rebid (3♣) which would mean rebidding 2♠ and concealing the club suit. (See Table 4.)
Very strong hands, up to about 20 points	If, for distributional reasons, a 20-point hand fails to qualify for better than an opening one-bid, it is unlikely to yield game unless facing a 'free' response from partner. If partner can respond at all, appropriate action can be taken on the next round by a jump to game or a game-forcing rebid.

TABLE 3 *(continued)*   13

Requirements	Comments
Examples:	
♠ A 4 ♥ A K Q ♦ A 4 3 2 ♣ Q 6 5 3	19 points. Open 1♦ and if partner makes *any* response, however weak, jump to 3NT.
♠ A 4 ♥ A K Q ♦ A 4 3 2 ♣ K 6 5 3	Open 2NT showing 20-22 points.
♠ K 6 4 ♥ A ♦ K Q 10 6 ♣ A Q J 9 8	Not qualified for better than a one-bid. Open 1♣ and if responder can bid at all, make a game-forcing jump rebid of 3♦ (1♣-1♥-3♦) showing 16+ points.

Note: Whether or not a minor suit reverse (1♣-1♥-2♦) is forcing is a matter of partnership agreement.

4-4-4-1 distribution with minimum of 13-14 points	With three biddable four-card suits open one of the suit below the singleton. UNLESS THE SINGLETON IS CLUBS, WHEN OPEN 1♥. If only two of the three suits qualify as biddable, bid as a two-suiter. Mentally demote the doubleton to a singleton and bid as above. 4-4-3-2 hands of less honour strength make dangerous opening bids as they have no playing strength unless partner can support.
Examples:	
♠ A J 10 6 ♥ 7 ♦ A J 4 2 ♣ K J 6 2	With three biddable 4-card suits and 14 honour points open 1♦. Trump shortage unless a fit in partner's hand is found is a disadvantage and discovery of this is best facilitated by opening one of the suit below the singleton.

TABLE 3 *(continued)*

Requirements	*Comments*
♠ A J 10 6 ♥ K J 6 2 ♦ A J 4 2 ♣ 7	With the club singleton open 1♥ over which responder could bid spades at the one-level. If he elects to bid 2♣ over 1♥, rebid 2♦.
♠ A K 10 6 ♥ A Q J 7 ♦ 7 ♣ 7 6 5 2	Ignore the club suit as being unbiddable except in support. Treat the hand as a major two-suiter and open 1♠. Over a response of 2♣ raise clubs or over 2♦ rebid 2♥.
♠ A J 9 2 ♥ Q 7 5 3 ♦ K Q 5 2 ♣ 8	With only a 4-4-4-1 distribution this hand is dangerously weak for an opening bid, as repeated attacks in clubs may cause declarer to lose all control. Pass originally, but support strongly if partner opens.

TABLE 4   15

Choice of Bids – Showing Shape

Division of suits	Order of bidding	Comments
5-5 or 6-6	If equal and adjacent, bid higher-ranking suit first unless both black, when bid clubs first.	The rules for opening bids are: 1 The longer suit before the shorter. 2 The higher-ranking before the lower. 3 The stronger suit before the weaker.
5-4	If adjacent, bid longer suit first on strong hands. If weak it may be necessary to bid 4-card suit first, to avoid reversing.	These rules are unavoidably over-lapping and conflicting, requiring judgement and experience for correct application. In general, MAKE THE MOST NATURAL BID AVAILABLE TAKING ALSO INTO ACCOUNT THE NEED FOR AN HONEST REBID.
6-5 7-6 7-5	Longer suit first unless hand is weak and shorter adjacent suit ranks higher. Rebid in shorter suit.	In bidding two suits you are offering partner a choice and he needs to know which you do, in fact, prefer.
6-4	Bid and repeat 6-card suit before bidding 4-card suit unless a 4-card major can be rebid at the one-level.	Provided a hand is strong enough for opener to wish to show two long suits, the normal bid of the longer suit first should be made. The shorter can then be bid *and rebid*. 1♥-1♠ 2♦-2♠ 3♦

Division of suits	Order of bidding	Comments
		Thus if a suit is worth a second bid when unsupported, it must be at least a 5-card suit. The first-bid suit must, therefore, be at least as long, or longer, than the second suit. Here opener is either 6-5 or 5-5 in hearts and diamonds.
4-4	With adjacent suits, higher ranking first. With spades and clubs, clubs first.	*Acol* avoids the use of prepared bids as far as possible, so if a natural bid is available, make it. Since bidding two suits implies a wish to be given preference by responder, a reverse bid, i.e., a bid in a low-ranking suit followed by one in a higher-ranking suit (1♥-2♦-2♠) indicates that the hand is strong enough for preference to be given at the three-level. NEVER REVERSE MERELY TO SHOW STRENGTH. 1♥-2♦ 2♠-3♥ If expedient a reverse may be made on a strong hand (16 or more points). The act of making a reverse bid, therefore, announces strength and shape. (See Table 19.) The first bid suit is guaranteed to be longer than the second.

TABLE 4 *(continued)* 17

Examples:

♠ 8
♥ A K 9 8 4
♦ A Q 10 6 4
♣ 8 3

With two equal and adjacent suits, open one of the higher-ranking, 1♥, giving a comfortable rebid of 2♦ over 1♠ or 2♣. Exchange the spades and hearts, and you must open 1♠ intending to rebid 2♦ over 2♣ but, if responder bids 2♥, you must rebid 2♠ as the hand is not strong enough for a forcing rebid of 3♦ (new suit at the three-level).

♠ 8
♥ A K 9 8 4 3
♦ A Q 10 6 4
♣ 8

Open 1♥, the 6-card suit and then bid and *rebid* in diamonds showing that, as the diamond suit is *rebiddable*, it is at least a 5-card suit. The first-bid suit, hearts, is likely to be at least as long, if not longer.

♠ A Q 10 9 2
♥ K J 9 7 5 4 3
♦ –
♣ A

This hand is extremely strong distributionally and well up to the values for a reverse. Open 1♥, the longer suit, and reverse into 2♠ over a response in either minor. This is a one-round force.

♠ 8
♥ A 10 9 7 6
♦ A J 8 7 6 5
♣ 8

Compare this much weaker hand which is not strong enough for an opening of 1♦ with a forcing reverse into 2♥ over a black suit response. Break Rule No. 1 and open 1♥ allowing for a simple rebid in diamonds.

♠ A Q 10 9 7
♥ K 3
♦ 8
♣ Q 10 8 5 3

With the two black suits of equal length open 1♣, allowing for a simple rebid of 1♠ (which does *not* constitute a reverse) over a red-suit response. It follows that you can also rebid 2♠ over partner's 1NT response without promising great strength.

♠ A Q 7 2
♥ 8
♦ A Q 9 8 6 3
♣ Q 2

Open 1 ♦, the 6-card suit. Repeat diamonds over a 1NT or 2♣ response. Over a response of 1 ♥, take the chance to bid the 4-card spade suit at the one-level. Again, not a strength showing reverse, but compare the sequence 1 ♦-2♣-2 ♥ (strength-showing) as there is never a chance of showing hearts at the one-level after a 1 ♦ bid.

♠ A K Q 9
♥ A Q J 9 7
♦ 7 4
♣ K 3

Open 1 ♥, the longer suit, and reverse into 2♠ over any response. The hearts are good enough to accept a preference into 3 ♥. Compare this, however, with this final example.

♠ A Q 9 4
♥ A J 10 8 7
♦ 7 3
♣ Q 4

Too strong not to open but not strong enough to bid 1 ♥ and reverse into 2♠. The choice is, therefore, between opening 1 ♥ and rebidding 2 ♥ over 2♣ or 2 ♦, or bidding the 4-card spade suit first allowing for a rebid of 2 ♥. The latter is the better choice.

TABLE 5   19

Simple Change-of-suit Responses

Range	Requirements	Comments
New suit at the one-level (1♥ – 1♠)	A minimum of 6 honour points with a biddable 4-card suit	A simple change-of-suit at the one-level is *forcing* unless responder has previously passed. Guarantees no more than 1NT response would do but may be much stronger – only just short of values for a game force.

Examples:

♠ A 10 8 7
♥ J 3 2
♦ J 10 6
♣ 8 6 5

If partner opens 1♣, 1♦ or 1♥, respond 1♠. Pass any rebid other than a force or if preference to partner's first bid suit is indicated, e.g. 1♥-1♠-2♣-2♥. The 2♥ rebid is simple preference and not a raise.

♠ J 10 8 7
♥ K 9 7 5 3
♦ J 7 3
♣ 5

If partner opens 1♣ or 1♦ respond 1♥. Note that if he opens one of either major the hand qualifies for a limit-bid in that suit (1♥-2♥ or 1♠-2♠) (see Table 7).

New suit at the two-level (1♥ – 2♦ or 1♠ – 2♥)	Minimum of 9 honour points	Holding a 6-card suit, the honour points may be reduced to 7. With a stronger responding hand a 4-card suit will suffice. 2♥ facing 1♠ guarantees a 5-card heart suit. *Never* bid 2♥ in response to 1♠ without at least a 5-card heart suit.

Examples:

♠ J 8 6
♥ K 8 7 5 4
♦ Q 8 6
♣ 7 2

Respond to 1♣ or 1♦ with 1♥, but not strong enough for 2♥ over 1♠ so respond 1NT. Replace the ♥8 with the ♥Q making 8 honour points and 2♥ may be bid in response to partner's 1♠.

♠ K 10 5 4 ♥ 5 3 ♦ A Q 8 7 ♣ K J 3	Opposite 1♥ bid 1♠. Opposite 1♠, too strong for a limit-bid which might be passed or for 4♠ (pre-emptive) which might mean a missed slam. Respond 2♦. If opener rebids 2♠ make a *delayed game raise* of 4♠ (see Table 22).
♠ Q 8 2 ♥ J 10 9 5 4 ♦ K Q 3 2 ♣ 8	Respond to 1♣ or 1♦ with 1♥. Respond to 1♠ with 2♥. If, having passed originally when partner opens 1♦, 1♥ would no longer be forcing, it costs nothing to bid 2♥, guaranteeing a raise to 3♦ but showing the hearts on the way.
♠ Q 10 8 ♥ 8 4 ♦ A J 9 8 6 2 ♣ 8 4	Respond 2♦ to 1♥ or 1♠. If opener rebids 3♣ (forcing) give simple preference to a spade opening. Compare the following:

a) N   S   b) N   S   c) N   S
   1♠ – 2♦   1♠ – 2♦   1♥ – 2♦
   2♥ – 2♠   3♣ – 3♠   3♣ – 3♦

In (a) give preference, as also in (b). In (c) the doubleton heart is inadequate to show preference when the 6-card suit can be rebid.

TABLE 6   21

Jump Take-out Responses

Range	Requirements	Comments
One level more than for simple take-out (1♥ – 2♠ or 1♥ – 3♣)	13-14 points and strong 6 or 7-card suit	Jump take-out into new suit is an *unconditional game force* – the strongest possible response. Shows game certain, slam possible. When the bulk of responder's values is in one strong suit, the jump take-out will avoid possible difficulties on the next round.
	With 16 or more honour points a force is mandatory except with complete lack of fit for partners	When forcing with a good fit in opener's suit, make the jump, if possible, in a suit which ranks below his. With a good fit, force immediately. With no fit, be more conservative. There are no arbitrary requirements laid down.

Examples:
♠6
♥A K 10 7 4
♦K Q 7 5
♣K Q 9

If partner opens 1♥, force with 3♦. If he opens 1♣ or 1♦, force with 2♥. If he opens 1♠ – an apparent misfit – bid 2♥ and await developments. Make the ♦Q into the ♠Q and there is no longer a misfit, so an immediate force is mandatory.

♠J 7 6
♥A K Q J 6 5 4
♦K 6
♣7

Over 1♣, 1♦ or 1♠, force with a jump bid in hearts and continue repeating hearts at each rebid. You may otherwise be in difficulty for an expressive rebid on the second round.

Range	Requirements	Comments
Two or more levels than for a simple take-out (1♥ – 3♠ or 1♥ – 4♠)	Long suit in weak hand (7-card suit or longer)	Pre-emptive, not forcing, to obstruct the opposition and also to warn partner that the hand must be played in responder's suit. Note: Pre-emptive bids to the four-level cannot be made in the minor suits over a major suit opening. (See Swiss Convention, Table 8.)

Examples:

♠ A 9 8 7 6 5 2
♥ 7 6
♦ 6 2
♣ 9 4

If partner opens 1♣, 1♦ or 1♥ bid 3♠ showing weakness except for spade length, which will be the only feature of the hand. Such pre-emptive action may well make it impossible for opponents to find their own best contract.

♠ 7
♥ K Q J 9 8 6 3 2
♦ 9 2
♣ 8 6

If partner opens 1♣, 1♦ or 1♠, bid 4♥, a contract you might even make, apart from making life difficult for opponents with spade ambitions. If the suit were either minor, jump direct to five as the four-level is conventional over a 1♥ or 1♠ opening (see Table 8).

Suit Limit-bid Responses

Raise	Requirements	Comments
Single raise of suit bid (1♥ – 2♥ or 1♦ – 2♦)	3-5 points with 5-card trump support or 5-9 points with 4-card support	The weakest possible response giving little more than the assurance of trump support whilst combining at least some pre-emptive effect. In the minors, the bid will generally deny a biddable major suit.
Examples: ♠9654 ♥9852 ♦K93 ♣K4		Raise an opening 1♥ or 1♠ to 2♥ or 2♠. In support of either major the hand counts 7 points, 6 in honours and one for the doubleton club.
♠84 ♥9862 ♦Q9873 ♣K2		Raise 1♥ to 2♥ or 1♦ to 2♦. Over 1♣ bid 1♦. Over 1♠ it might well turn out best to pass, which will depend on factors such as the state of the score, position at the table, etc. If you decide to respond, bid 1NT, not a suit.
Double raise of suit bid (1♠ – 3♠ or 1♣ – 3♣)	In the majors, 5-card trump support, 7-10 points, and shape, or 4-card trump support and 10-12 points. In the minors, 10-12 points.	A non-forcing but highly encouraging limit-bid, approximately equivalent to a 2NT response though guaranteeing trump support. In the minors, the bid will usually deny a 4-card major and is likely to be taken as an invitation to 3NT. For this reason the count should not be devalued unless responder is prepared to remove 3NT into four, or even five, of the minor.

Examples:

♠ K J 7 3
♥ Q 9 3
♦ J 9 7 2
♣ K 6

Raise 1♠ to 3♠ on 10 honour + 1 distributional point. Over an opening of 1♣, 1♦ or 1♥, bid 1♠ unless having previously passed when, over 1♦, it costs nothing to bid 2♠, guaranteeing a raise to 3♦ but showing spades on the way. 1♠ would no longer be forcing and might be passed.

♠ K 7
♥ J 9 3 2
♦ A Q 9 7 6
♣ 9 2

Over 1♣ bid 1♦. Over 1♠ bid 2♦. Over 1♦ bid 1♥. Over 1♥ bid 2♦ first to give partner more information about your hand, so that he will be better placed to judge whether to go higher.

♠ K J 3
♥ Q 9 2
♦ J 9 8 7
♣ K J 3

See Table 9 as this hand makes a good 2NT response to any one-level suit opening, including 1♦. It is also likely to play better with the lead coming up to, rather than through it, and the diamond fit will help in establishing the suit.

♠ Q 7
♥ K J 9 8
♦ K 8 7 4 3
♣ K 3

Compare this hand. Raise 1♥ to 3♥. Bid 1♦ over 1♣, 2♦ over 1♠, or 1♥ over 1♦.

TABLE 8   25

Direct Raise to Game and Swiss

Raise	Requirements	Comments
Direct jump to game (1♥ – 4♥ or 1♦ – 5♦)	In the majors about 5 points. In the minors about 8 points.	Shows exceptional trump support with low honour count but shape by way of voids or singletons. Highly pre-emptive though there may be a possible play for game on distribution.

Examples:

♠ J 9 7 6 4
♥ 6
♦ 8 2
♣ K Q 10 6 3

Worth a raise of 1♠ direct to 4♠, a highly pre-emptive bid which may keep opponents out of the auction. Note the useful side suit which might be established for discards, and also the red-suit shortages.

♠ 6
♥ 8 2
♦ Q 9 7 6 5 4
♣ K Q J 6

Worth a raise of 1♦ direct to 5♦ which may keep opponents out of the auction. In a competitive situation too it may prevent investigations, e.g. if the opening has been overcalled with 1♥ or 1♠, 5♦ may make it impossible for the over-caller's partner to judge his best course of action.

| Swiss Convention: 1♥ – 4♣ or 1♠ – 4♣ | At least 4-card trump support and *two aces* | These conventional responses do *not* replace forcing bids if the strength for these is held, but show hands with specific controls and trump support. As they ensure at least a game contract, suitable hands must contain about 13-15 points. A simple conversion to the major-suit game by opener should be passed. Over either |
| 1♥ – 4♦ or 1♠ – 4♦ | At least 4-card trump support and *three aces* | |

Raise	Requirements	Comments
		4♣ or 4♦ (or in the sequence 1♠-4♣-4♦-4♠) 4NT by opener is the *Acol direct king convention* (see Table 42).

Examples:

♠ Q J 10 7
♥ A J 9 2
♦ 8 4
♣ A J 8

If partner opens either 1♥ or 1♠ bid 4♣, agreeing the trump suit and showing two aces. Note that the hand is below strength for a jump take-out into a new suit. If partner rebids 4NT he is asking for kings on the Blackwood scale (not aces, which he already knows).

♠ A J 10 7
♥ A J 9 2
♦ 8 4
♣ A J 8

If partner opens 1♥ or 1♠ bid 4♦, agreeing the trump suit and showing three aces. If partner now bids 4NT respond 5♣ to show no *kings* on the Blackwood scale.

♠ Q J 10 7
♥ A J 9
♦ 8 2
♣ A J 8 4

If partner opens 1♠ respond 4♣, agreeing spades as trumps and showing 13-15 points and two aces. If partner opens any other suit a Swiss bid is not available.

Note: There are many versions of the Swiss convention and one of the latest is Fruit Machine Swiss. In response to 1♥ or 1♠, 4♣ is a three-way bid, showing either two aces and a singleton or three aces, or two aces and the king of trumps.

TABLE 9   27

No-trump Limit-bids in Response

Bidding	Requirements	Comments
1♥ – 1NT or 1♠ – 1NT	6-9 points, with insufficient trump support for suit raise	A weak limit-bid denying 4-card trump support *or* the values to bid a new suit at the two-level. A response to be avoided on as good as 9 points if any other bid can be found.
1♣ – 1NT	8-10 points, which may include a 4-card club fit	Over an opening 1♣ any other suit can be shown at the one-level. It therefore becomes more constructive to reserve 1NT as a positive count-showing response, not merely to keep open.
1♦ – 1NT	As above, but 6-9 points	Bid 1NT if you have no 4-card major.

Examples:

♠Q87
♥K85
♦Q63
♣Q954

Respond 1NT to any one-level opening bid, *but* exchange the ♠Q for the ♠9 and over 1♦, 1♥ or 1♠ the response should be 1NT but 1♣ should be raised to 2♣ as the hand would no longer be strong enough to bid 1NT.

♠Q6
♥764
♦J10976
♣KJ6

If partner opens 1♥ or 1♠ bid 1NT, not 2♦ which would promise 8 points or more. Over 1♣ respond 1♦ or raise 1♦ to 2♦.

Bidding	Requirements	Comments
1♣ – 2NT 1♦ – 2NT 1♥ – 2NT 1♠ – 2NT	11-12 honour points in a balanced hand	Approximately equivalent to a suit limit-bid to the three-level. Except possibly in the minors *denies* 4-card trump support though there should be at least a doubleton in the suit opened by partner. Denies a 4-card major bid-dable at the one-level.

Examples:

♠ J 10 8
♥ K 6 4
♦ K J 4
♣ Q J 7 6

Over a one-level opening bid in any suit, bid 2NT. Exchange the ♠8 for a fourth diamond, and the spade stop would be inadequate for 2NT except over a 1♠ opening, and it would be better to make a temporising bid in a minor suit.

♠ K Q 8
♥ A 3
♦ 7 3
♣ Q J 7 6 4 2

Not suitable for a 2NT response to any opening bid. Clubs may safely be bid at the two-level and then, if partner's bidding suggests a hold on diamonds, rebid 2NT which still shows the 10-12 count.

Bidding	Requirements	Comments
3NT in response to any opening one bid	13-15 honour points in a balanced hand with no good alternative bid	A strong limit-bid, *not* a shut-out. If opener is himself strong he should be encouraged to make slam investigations. A response to be avoided if a more constructive one is available as it uses what may be valuable bidding space. Sometimes it is impossible to find another appropriate bid.

TABLE 9 *(continued)*   29

Examples:

♠ A Q 9
♥ J 10 3
♦ Q J 7
♣ Q J 8 5

Whichever suit partner opens there is no descriptive response other than 3NT. Neither spades nor the red suits can be raised directly, a raise of 1♣ to 3♣ risks being passed, and any higher bid would exclude the 3NT level.

♠ A Q 9
♥ J 10 7 6
♦ A Q 8
♣ Q 7 6

If partner opens 1♣ or 1♦ bid a temporising 1♥. If he opens 1♥ bid a Swiss 4♣ (see Table 8). If he opens 1♠, however, the hand is not suitable for a 2♥ response and by far the most descriptive bid is an immediate 3NT.

Conventional No-trump Responses

Response	Comments
4NT in response to any opening suit bid	The immediate use of your chosen slam convention. By inference agrees partner's trump suit, but should only be used when there is no need for bidding space to investigate the best final denomination. The normal Blackwood responses are required.
5NT in response to any opening suit bid	*Grand slam force*, showing responder's interest *only* in the three top honours in suit opened. Acol advocates the use of the modified convention whereby a bid of 5NT, if not preceded by 4NT, asks partner to show *how many* of the three top trump honours he holds. The responses are, with none (a knave-high suit) 6♣, with one (ace, king or queen) 6 of the trump suit, and with any two of the three, 7 of the trump suit. Thus a player who holds two of the three himself can discover whether partner holds the missing one required for the grand slam contract.
Example: ♠ A K 3 ♥ Q J 10 7 6 ♦ 7 6 ♣ A K Q or ♠ A K 3 ♥ Q J 10 7 6 ♦ – ♣ A K Q J 10	If partner opens 1♥, it is vital that his ace-holding should be checked before either a small or grand slam is bid. So respond 4NT, agreeing hearts as trumps and, if opener shows two aces, follow with 5NT to ask for kings. Exchange the ♦ 7 6 for the ♣ J 10, and the grand slam is a certainty if opener holds his own ♥ A K. Bid a direct 5NT, ensuring that you will stay out of the grand slam if he only has one of these two honours.

TABLE 11 31

One No-trump Opening Bids and Direct Raises

Opener's points	Responder raises	Opener's rebid	Comments
1NT weak, 12-14 points, balanced hand	To 2NT on 11-12 points	Pass on 12 points	ALL NO-TRUMP OPENINGS, RESPONSES OR REBIDS, unless conventional, ARE LIMIT-BIDS MADE ON CLEARLY DEFINED COUNTS WITHIN NARROW LIMITS.
	To 3NT on 12+ points	Bid 3NT on 13-14 points	
1NT strong, 15-17 points	To 2NT on 8-9 points	Pass on 15 points	Values for raises and rebids are based on the probability that 25-26 points between two evenly-balanced hands, or 24 points, with a 5-card suit, will yield nine tricks at no-trumps. As responder, add points to the opener's known minimum. If this totals 22 or 23, raise to 2NT inviting opener to bid 3NT if better than minimum. If the total reaches 24-25points, bid 3NT direct.
	To 3NT on 9+ points	Bid 3NT on 16-17 points	

Prepared minor-suit openings may occasionally be needed to complement the point counts required for no-trump openings. Optional alternatives for NT openings are weak throughout, i.e. 12-14 points at all times, or variable, 12-14 points if not vulnerable and 15-17 if vulnerable.

TABLE 11 *(continued)*

Examples:

♠ Q 10 3
♥ A J 9 4
♦ K 8 2
♣ K 9 8

A typical weak (12-14 point) 1NT opener, avoiding any rebid problems. If using a strong no-trump the choice is between passing (unthinkable!) or bidding a prepared 1♣, as to open 1♥ would give no honest rebid over 2♣ or 2♦.

♠ K 8 6
♥ Q 10 5
♦ Q 7 3
♣ A K 10 9

1♣ is the only available opening if using a 15-17 point no-trump. If using a 12-14 point no-trump, this opening gives a good picture of the hand as well as avoiding any problem as to an honest rebid.

♠ K J 7
♥ Q 10 8
♦ A 10 7 3
♣ K Q 6

Open 1NT if using strong on this hand. If using weak, the count is too high, but it is safe to open 1♦, prepared to rebid 1NT over a major-suit response, or 2NT over a 2♣ response (see Table 16).

♠ Q 10 6
♥ K 8 5
♦ A 9 8 7
♣ J 9 8

As responder, if partner opens 1NT weak, pass. Even added to his possible maximum of 14 points, the combined count cannot reach game values. As responder to a strong no-trump, raise to 3NT direct. 15 + 10 ½ = 25 ½ = game values.

♠ K 9 6
♥ K 8 5
♦ A 10 8 7
♣ J 10 9

Raise partner's opening 12-14 point no-trump to 2NT. With 10s counting ½ point in no-trump bidding, the combined count cannot be less than 24. Raise a strong no-trump direct to 3NT. Replace ♣J with ♣Q and raise even a weak no-trump direct to 3NT.

Note: Direct quantitative raises to the higher levels (based on the combined minimum known to responder to be held) may be made as set out at the head of Table 23.

TABLE 12   33

Prepared Openings of 1♣ or 1♦

Openings of 1♣ or 1♦ are more likely to be natural than prepared but occasionally, because of the agreed strength of the opening no-trump, one must 'prepare' so as to ensure an honest rebid.

The incidence of prepared 1♣ or 1♦ openings is considerably lower if using a 12-14 point no-trump throughout than if using 15-17 points, as usually a 15-point hand can be opened with a bid of its 4-card suit and rebid in no-trumps at the lowest available level.

If a prepared opening is unavoidable, choose a 3-card minor headed by at least one of the three top honours. If both minors qualify, open 1♣, not 1♦. After the prepared opening, the rebid should always be in no-trumps unless responder bids opener's 4-card suit, which may be raised.

NEVER USE A PREPARED 1♣ OR 1♦ OPENING IF THE HAND CONTAINS A NATURAL BID ALLOWING FOR AN HONEST REBID.

Examples:

♠ K J 3
♥ A 9 8 6
♦ Q J 9
♣ K 10 9

Open 1NT if using 12-14 points. If using 15-17 points, open 1♣ as the hand is not strong enough to open 1♥ and rebid 2NT if partner responds 2♣ or 2♦. Having opened 1♣, rebid 1NT over 1♦ or 1♠, but raise 1♥ to 2♥.

♠ K Q 3
♥ 8 7 6 5
♦ A J 9
♣ A J 7

Open 1NT if using 15-17 points but, if using 12-14 points, the heart holding is too scanty to consider bidding except in support. Open 1♣ and rebid 1NT unless partner bids 1♥, which raise.

♠ A K 3 ♥ A 9 6 2 ♦ K J 8 ♣ 8 6 4	An uncomfortable hand for an opening 1NT whatever strength is being used. Also uncomfortable if opened 1♣ and responder bids 1♦ or 1♠. Open 1♦, *not* 1♣, and raise either major suit response. Bid 2NT over a 2♣ response.
♠ A Q 8 3 ♥ Q 7 5 ♦ Q 10 8 ♣ K 9 7	Open 1NT (12-14). If using 15-17 points open 1♣ and rebid 1NT, *not* 1♠, over a red-suit response. A spade rebid would indicate a black two-suiter which might lead to a disastrous final contract.
♠ 8 7 6 5 ♥ 10 6 5 4 ♦ A K 8 ♣ A K	Open 1NT (12-14). If interested in a major suit fit responder will bid 2♣ (see Table 14); a fit will not, therefore, be missed. Open 1♦ (15-17) and raise either major if bid by responder. Exchange the ♥10 for the ♥J and these two sequences would be reversed.
♠ K 7 ♥ 9 7 6 ♦ A 7 ♣ A Q J 8 7 5	A perfectly natural 1♣ opening (or 1♦ if these suits were reversed) which would be shown by a rebid in the suit opened.

TABLE 13   35

Suit Responses to 1NT Openings

Response	Requirements	Comments
2♣		Conventional (see Table 14).
2♦, 2♥ or 2♠	Weak hand lacking game values but with a 5- or 6-card suit	Values depend on known strength of opening no-trump bid, e.g. 8 points is weak facing a 12-14 point no-trump but worth a game contract facing 15-17 points.
		A response of 2♦, 2♥ or 2♠ is *a weak take-out* and opener should not rebid except competitively, or, very occasionally, invitationally to the three-level, if holding a maximum count and good trump fit.

Examples:

♠6 ♥QJ9752 ♦J1053 ♣85	A worthless hand if played in no-trumps but the 6-card suit, if used as trumps, *must* be an improvement. Facing either a weak or a strong no-trump, bid 2♥, which you have a better chance of coming near to making than 1NT.
♠K96542 ♥72 ♦A86 ♣94	It would need more than ordinary good fortune to make a game if facing a weak no-trump so take out into 2♠ which may even make with an overtrick. Facing a strong no-trump, however, it is worth a game try (see over).

TABLE 13 *(continued)*

Response	Requirements	Comments
3♥ or 3♠	Game values favouring a suit contract	Emphasis on preference for a suit contract, i.e. an unbalanced hand. Opener should raise suit with 3-card support or bid 3NT with a doubleton.
3♣ or 3♦	Reserved for a slam try	Responder's strength will, of course, vary with known strength of opening no-trump.

Examples:

♠ K Q 9 8 7 6
♥ A Q 5
♦ 8
♣ Q 7 6

Clearly worth a game contract whichever strength of opening no-trump is being used, so bid 3♠ and take out a 3NT conversion into 4♠. Don't bid 4♠ direct, which indicates a somewhat different type of hand.

♠ K Q 10
♥ A Q 5
♦ K J 10 9 8
♣ 8 3

Bid 3NT in response to a weak 1NT. Opposite a strong 1NT bid a slam try of 3♦.

4♥, 4♠, 5♣ or 5♦	Extremely unbalanced hand with at least 7-card suit	The count will again vary according to the known strength of the opening bid, but the hand should be worthless except for a possible game in the suit bid. Intended as both highly pre-emptive and as a warning to opener not to bid again.

TABLE 13 *(continued)*   37

Response	Requirements	Comments
Example: ♠ 9 ♥ 8 6 ♦ A 6 ♣ K Q 9 8 6 5 3 2		Unattractive unless played in clubs. Facing a strong no-trump, bid 3♣ but, facing a weak no-trump, and also having regard to the extreme weakness in both majors, a direct jump to 5♣ may well produce the best result.
4♣	Any strong	Conventional Gerber slam try. See Table 24.

TABLE 14
1NT – 2♣ (Fit-finding)

Requirements	Comments
An unbalanced hand, weak or strong, hoping to find a major suit fit	2♣ in response to 1NT is conventional and unlimited and is used to investigate a major-suit fit with opener's hand for either part-score or game contracts. The convention should *not* be used if responder is not sensibly prepared for any opener's rebid, and should normally be confined to hands best suited to a major-suit contract. 2♣ requests opener to show any 4-card major suit held. With one he bids it at the two-level. With two he bids the hearts first. With neither he bids 2♦ *irrespective of his point count or diamond holding.*

Summary:

1 Bid 2♣ in response to an opening 1NT whenever it seems wise to seek a suit fit, either for game or part-score.

2 First make sure that the hand contains a sensible second-round bid or pass, *whatever opener's response.*

3 If the desired fit is found, responder may, according to strength and the known value of the opening no-trump, either pass, raise invitationally to the three-level, or bid game direct.

4 If the desired fit is *not* found, a two-level rebid by responder becomes a weak take-out, to be passed by opener. A conversion to 2 or 3NT by responder shows the values in spite of lack of suit fit.

5 Following opener's 2♦ rebid, a jump to the three-level in a major (or a three-level bid in the *other* major if the rebid has been 2♥ or 2♠) is *highly invitational but non-forcing.*

6 Following opener's 2♦ rebid, a responder's rebid of 3♦ is *unconditionally forcing* and requests opener to show his better major, preferring length to strength. (Extended Stayman.)

TABLE 14 *(continued)* 39

IMPORTANT: There is no point-count limit for the 2♣ bidder, the only requirement being the possession of a sensible rebid, which generally means a sensible course of action if opener rebids 2♦.

Examples:

♠ Q 10 9 6
♥ A 8 5 4
♦ 8
♣ K Q 6 4

The singleton makes this hand better fitted for a suit contract than for no-trumps. Bid 2♣ and raise opener's rebid of 2♥ or 2♠ to game. If opener rebids 2♦ bid 2NT over a weak no-trump and 3NT over a strong no-trump.

♠ J 10 8 5
♥ J 9 7 6 4
♦ 7 6 5
♣ 9

Instead of making the immediate weak take-out into 2♥, bid 2♣. If opener rebids either 2♥ or 2♠, *pass*. If he bids 2♦ bid 2♥, which now becomes the weak take-out you could have made on the first round.

♠ Q 9 8 5
♥ J 10 7 4
♦ 9 7 6 5 3
♣ –

Bid 2♣ facing 1NT and pass any opener's rebid *including* 2♦. You could have made a 2♦ weak take-out in the first place if you were lacking the machinery to investigate a spade or heart fit.

♠ J 8
♥ 9 7 6
♦ K 3
♣ Q J 9 6 5 4

Bid 2♣, which opener will take as a request to show a 4-card major if he has one. Over his rebid, respond 3♣, to show the long club suit in a weak hand unsuitable for a no-trump contract. Opener will now pass.

♠ 10 9 7 6
♥ 7
♦ Q 8
♣ Q J 9 6 5 4

Bid 2♣, which again opener will take as a request to show a 4-card major if he has one. If he rebids 2♠, pass, having discovered a 4-4 fit. If he bids 2♦ or 2♥, rebid 3♣ as in the previous example.

| ♠ Q 9 8 7
♥ Q 8 5 3
♦ 8
♣ Q 9 7 4 | Although you would prefer to find a suit fit, you have no sensible course of action available if you bid 2♣ and opener rebids 2♦. Either 2♥ or 2♠ would be idiotic in the face of at best a 4-3 fit, and to rebid 2NT, which would show the values for this initial response, would be grossly untrue, so *pass*. |

NEVER USE THE 2♣ FIT-FINDING CONVENTION ON A BALANCED HAND SUITABLE FOR A TRUMP CONTRACT UNLESS USING THE 'SID CONVENTION' – SEE PAGE 41. On such hands, either pass or give the appropriate direct raise in no-trumps. The 2♣ bid seeks the best final denomination. Note the following examples covering this and other points:

♠ 9 8 7 6 ♥ Q 9 8 ♦ K J 3 ♣ K 9 7	This evenly-balanced hand is likely to play as well in no-trumps as in a suit. Pass an opening 12-14 point no-trump, but raise a 15-17 point no-trump direct to 3NT. No enquiry as to the best denomination is needed.
♠ K Q 10 9 7 4 ♥ A Q 9 6 ♦ 4 ♣ 8 3	Bid 2♣ facing 1NT. If opener rebids either 2♥ or 2♠, raise direct to game. If he bids 2♦ bid 4♠ *direct* as you want to play in game anyway and, on partner's opening, are assured of at least a 2-card fit for spades.
♠ J 9 7 2 ♥ A Q J 9 3 ♦ A 3 ♣ 7 2	Bid 2♣ facing 1NT (weak), and raise an opener's rebid in either major direct to game. If partner rebids 2♦ bid 3♥, *highly invitational but non-forcing* showing values just short of the ability to force on the first round.

TABLE 14 *(continued)* 41

♠ K Q 10 9 7 ♥ A Q 6 5 ♦ 4 ♣ Q 3 2	1NT – 2♣ 2♦ – 3♦ ?	Responder's 3♦ rebid is *unconditionally forcing* and is a conventional demand for opener, who has already denied a 4-card major, to show his *better* major, preferring length to strength.
♠ J 9 7 ♥ A J 9 8 3 2 ♦ 6 ♣ K J 5	1NT – 2♣ 2♠ – 3♥ ?	This responder's hand is worth a game contract if a heart fit exists so bid 2♣. If opener rebids either 2♦ or 2♠, rebid 3♥, again highly invitational but not forcing. Opener may pass 3♥, raise to 4♥, or convert to 3NT.

SID (STAYMAN IN DOUBT)

♠ 8 3 2 ♥ K Q 9 4 ♦ A Q J ♣ 7 6 4	1NT – 2♣ 2♥ – 3♦ ?	Responder's hand is worth a game contract but two suits are weak. 2♣ reveals heart fit. Now over 2♥, 3♦ shows game values, heart fit, and a flat hand with *no ruffing values*. Opener must now choose between 3NT and 4♥, and will choose 4♥ if he holds a losing doubleton in another suit.

Opener's Rebids after No-trump Opening

Responder's bids will, of course, be based on the known values of the opening no-trump. Opener's rebids are as follows:

Bidding	Opener's rebids	Examples
1NT – 2NT ?	Pass on minimum holding but accept invitation to bid game on a good medium or a maximum. Here, with 12 ½ points, pass but add even the ♦J and opener should raise to 3NT.	♠ Q J 7 ♥ K 9 3 ♦ A 9 8 3 ♣ Q 10 9
1NT – 2♦ or 2♥ or 2♠ ?	Pass as responder has made a weak take-out. Just very occasionally, with good trump fit and a maximum, opener may bid an invitational three of the suit, as 3♥ on this hand.	♠ A 6 ♥ A Q 9 2 ♦ A 9 8 7 ♣ 9 8 7
1NT – 2♣ ?	Show any 4-card major suit held. With both bid hearts first. With neither, bid 2♦ *irrespective* of point count or diamond holding. Here bid 2♥ in response to 2♣.	♠ K 9 2 ♥ 10 8 7 2 ♦ A Q 7 ♣ Q J 6
1NT – 2♣ 2♥ – 3♥ ?	On maximum hand and good trump fit, accept responder's invitation (not force) and bid 4♥. His hand will be just short of the values to bid 4♥ direct.	♠ K 9 2 ♥ Q 8 7 2 ♦ A Q 7 ♣ Q J 6

TABLE 15 *(continued)*   43

Bidding	Opener's rebids	Examples
1NT – 3♥ ?	Responder's 3♥ (or any three-level jump) is an unconditional game force on a hand better fitted for a suit contract. With a 3-card fit raise to game in the suit. With a poorer fit, rebid 3NT.	♠ K 9 2 ♥ Q 8 7 ♦ A Q 7 ♣ Q 9 8 2
1NT – 3♥ ?	An exception to the previous example – if opener is *maximum* and has a good trump fit, he may show mild slam ambitions by an *advance cue-bid*. Here he may respond to the 3♥ force by bidding 3♠ which agrees hearts as trumps, shows 14 points (max) and the ♠A. Pass if responder converts to 4♥.	♠ A 7 6 ♥ K J 9 6 ♦ K Q 6 ♣ J 7 2
1NT – 2♣ 2♥ – 3♠ ?	When responder has bid 2♣ and his subsequent bid, though not a weak take-out, indicates that the desired fit has not been found, his three-level bid is invitational, not forcing. Here opener has a good quality maximum and should raise to 4♠. Would also apply if opener's rebid had been 2♦ or in the sequence 1NT-2♣-2♠-3♥.	♠ K 7 2 ♥ A Q 8 2 ♦ A 10 9 ♣ J 10 9
1NT – 2♣ 2♦ – 3♦	Responder's 3♦ rebid is *unconditionally forcing* and requires opener, who has denied a 4-card major, to show his better major, preferring length to strength. Here, of two 3-card majors, the hearts have the better honour content so bid 3♥, (Extended Stayman).	♠ K 7 2 ♥ K J 4 ♦ A 9 8 7 ♣ Q 10 7

Opener's No-trump Rebids after Suit Response

Bidding	Comments	Examples
At one-level: 1♦–1♥ 1NT	Shows 15-16 points unsuitable for a 1NT opening, either because too weak for strong no-trump or too strong for weak no-trump, or with gap that the response may have filled.	♠ A K 6 ♥ 7 2 ♦ A Q 9 6 ♣ Q 9 8 3
Over one-level bid: 1♥–1♠ 2NT	Shows balanced 17-18 points (or *good* 16). A strong though non-forcing limit-bid over which responder is expected to judge the best final contract, either game or part-score.	♠ K 7 ♥ A Q 9 5 ♦ K J 8 6 ♣ K J 3
1♥–1♠ 3NT	Shows balanced 19 points (20 points would have been opened 2NT). Not a shut-out bid and responder may convert to suit contract or make slam try if indicated on strength shown.	♠ Q 8 6 ♥ A K 7 3 ♦ K J 8 ♣ A Q 9
Over two-level bid: 1♥–2♦ 2NT	Lower values required for opener's rebid because of *greater* values promised by the two-level response. 2NT rebid is made on 15-16 points.	♠ K Q 6 ♥ A Q J 3 ♦ J 7 ♣ Q 10 8 3
1♥–2♦ 3NT	Similarly, for 3NT rebid, opener's hand can be scaled down to 17-18 points.	♠ K J 8 ♥ A K 7 3 ♦ J 8 7 ♣ A Q 9

TABLE 17   45

Opener's No-trump Rebids after 1NT Response

Bidding	Comments	Examples
1♥ – 1NT Pass	Opener may pass if no satisfactory alternative to 1NT presents itself, either by way of a suit rebid, or a new suit bid. Here 1NT should be as good a contract as any other.	♠ J 10 7 ♥ A K J 8 5 ♦ K 7 ♣ Q 9 8
1♥ – 1NT 2NT	Invitational bid to show balanced hand of 17-18 points. Responder may pass if minimum or raise to 3NT if prospects seem good. (See Table 9 for responder's values.)	♠ K 9 8 ♥ A Q J 7 ♦ J 10 7 ♣ A Q 4
1♥ – 1NT 3NT	Shows approximately 19 points or long suit which may be run to bring in nine tricks (the latter generally in a minor suit). Unwilling to miss game even if responder can only bid 1NT. If responder bids 2NT originally, opener judges his rebid against the 10-12 points promised by responder.	♠ K 9 8 ♥ A Q J 7 ♦ K J 7 ♣ A J 7

TABLE 18

Opener's Suit Rebids after No-trump Response

Bidding	Comments	Examples
1♥ – 1NT 2♥ or 1♥ – 1NT 2♦	Opener judges his rebid according to the strength shown by responder. Over 1NT any lowest-available-level rebid, either repeat of original suit or new suit, should be passed by responder except if preference is indicated. On the first example opener signs off in 2♥ and on the second shows his diamond suit which responder can pass or give preference to 2♥.	♠ A 9 3 ♥ Q J 9 8 6 2 ♦ K 7 4 ♣ 6 ♠ A 9 6 ♥ K J 9 6 2 ♦ K Q 9 7 4 ♣ –
1♥ – 1NT 3♥	A jump rebid of opener's suit is highly invitational but non-forcing. Though it may be passed, it asks responder to bid 4♥ or 3NT if his original response is maximum. Shows seven playing tricks at the suit bid.	♠ 10 ♥ A K J 9 8 7 ♦ A J 7 ♣ K 10 3
1♥ – 2NT 3♥ or 1♥ – 2NT Pass	Opener's repeat of his suit at the lowest available level is still a sign-off, judged in the light of the values shown by responder. Alternatively opener could pass the non-forcing 2NT limit-bid if this is judged wisest.	♠ A 9 3 ♥ Q J 9 8 6 2 ♦ K 7 4 ♣ 6

TABLE 18 *(continued)* 47

Bidding	Comments	Examples
1♥ – 2NT 3♦	Opener's change of suit rebid at the three-level is a *one-round force*, so responder must bid again. A mere preference to 3♥ over 3♦ can be passed by opener so responder should bid game if indicated.	♠ 7 ♥ K J 9 7 6 ♦ A K 10 7 ♣ A K 3
1♥ – 2NT 4♥ 1♥ – 2NT 3NT	As in rebidding after any other no-trump limit-bid, opener is expected to judge his hand against the values shown by responder. He may make a one-round force, as above, pass or sign off in three of his suit or, if strong enough, raise to 3NT or bid game direct in his own good suit. On the first example he should bid 4♥ and on the second should raise to 3NT.	♠ A 7 ♥ A Q J 9 8 5 ♦ Q 9 ♣ K 10 6 ♠ K 7 ♥ A Q 9 7 6 ♦ K J 8 ♣ K 10 6

TABLE 19

Opener's Suit Rebids after Change-of-suit Response

Bidding	Comments	Examples
1♥ – 1♠ 2♥ or 1♥ – 1♠ 2♦	Over a simple change-of-suit response, a repeat of opener's suit at the lowest available level is a sign-off. Similarly a weak two-suited hand may be shown by no higher than a two-level rebid in the second suit. Neither rebid is forcing and responder will pass unless he wishes to give preference and/or show additional values. Opener must bear this need for a rebid in mind before deciding to open a weak hand *unless* responder has previously passed.	♠ 8 ♥ K Q 9 8 7 6 ♦ 9 8 4 ♣ A J 10 or ♠ 8 ♥ A J 9 8 6 ♦ K Q J 6 3 ♣ Q 9
1♥ – 1♠ 3♥	A non-forcing invitational jump limit-bid asking responder to advance to game if his original bid is even fractionally better than minimum. Shows seven playing tricks at the suit named.	♠ 9 7 ♥ A K J 9 7 5 ♦ K J 8 ♣ A 7
1 – 2♥ 3♥	A simple raise of responder's bid suit shows trump support in a hand unsuitable for a stronger rebid. A non-forcing limit-bid denying the values to bid game direct.	♠ A Q 10 4 2 ♥ K Q 9 ♦ J 7 3 ♣ K 8
1♠ – 2♥ 4♥	The jump to game in responder's suit speaks for itself, showing that opener is unwilling to play below game level even if responder is minimum. Limited only by the fact that opener bid game instead of making a forcing rebid.	♠ A Q 10 4 2 ♥ K Q 9 7 ♦ J 7 ♣ K 8

TABLE 19 *(continued)* 49

Bidding	Comments	Examples
1♥ – 2♦ 3♣	A new suit rebid at the three-level is an unconditional force. It shows a hand which, facing a responder who can bid at the two-level, is worth a game contract.	♠ K 3 ♥ A Q J 8 6 ♦ A 7 ♣ K Q 10 7
1♥ – 1♠ 3♣	Over a one-level response, since a two-level rebid would be non-forcing, opener uses a jump rebid in a new suit if he wishes to force. The three-level rebid need not show an actual biddable suit, being used to ask responder to clarify his hand. Shows 16+ points.	♠ K Q 9 ♥ A Q J 8 6 ♦ K 9 ♣ A 10 9
1♥ – 2♣ 2♠	Opener's 2♠, a rebid in a suit higher-ranking than his first bid suit, which prevents responder from showing a preference at the two-level, is a *strength-showing reverse.* Modern practice regards this as a one-round force, though it is as well to have clear partnership under-standing. The first bid suit *must be* longer than the second.	♠ A K J 9 ♥ K Q J 10 5 ♦ 8 ♣ K 10 7
1♦ – 1♥ 1♠	Opener's rebid at the one-level does not constitute a forcing reverse; nor does a 1♣ opening followed by a 1♠ rebid (see Table 4 on Choice of Bid).	♠ A Q 6 2 ♥ 7 ♦ A Q 10 7 4 2 ♣ J 3

Opener's Rebid following Game-forcing Response

If partner makes a forcing jump take-out response (see Table 6), opener should seek to clarify his hand. The bidding cannot now be dropped below game level by either partner. It is safe, therefore, for opener to show any additional feature his hand may possess. For the most part, this will mean rebidding as he would have done over a simple response, except that it will be at the forced higher level.

Bidding	Comments	Examples
1♦ – 2♥ 2NT	Shows a 15-16 point hand on which opener had intended to rebid 1NT in a simple sequence. Now he is forced to the two-level to give the	♠ K J 5 ♥ J 9 8 ♦ K Q 8 4 ♣ A J 6
1♦ – 2♥ 3NT	same message. It follows that, had he intended to rebid 2NT in a simple sequence, he must not now do so. He must rebid 3NT to show his added values. This is *not* a stop-bid and responder may now continue with slam investigations if he thinks his hand warrants it.	♠ K J 5 ♥ J 9 8 ♦ A Q 8 4 ♣ A Q 6
1♦ – 2♥ 3♦	A repeat of opener's suit at the forced higher level confirms length and also that the hand has no other feature worth showing.	♠ 8 4 ♥ K 7 ♦ K J 9 8 6 5 ♣ A 9 3
1♦ – 2♥ 3♥	Good support for the suit in which partner forces must, of course, be shown by a raise in the suit. Don't cramp the bidding by making a jump to game – be content to agree the suit.	♠ 8 ♥ K J 9 8 ♦ K J 9 8 6 5 ♣ A 9

TABLE 20 *(continued)* 51

Bidding	Comments	Examples
1♥ – 2♠ 3♣	Over a forcing response opener should take this early opportunity to show any second biddable suit. The 3♣ rebid shows no more strength than would be needed for 2♣ in a simple sequence.	♠ K 4 ♥ A Q 9 7 6 ♦ 7 4 ♣ K Q J 9
1♠ – 3♦ 4♠	The jump rebid when a forcing situation is in being is conventional. Compare the third example on p.50, when a simple rebid at the three-level merely confirmed suit length (see below).	♠ A K Q J 9 3 ♥ 10 9 7 5 ♦ A 6 ♣ 7
1♦ – 2♥ 4♦	The jump rebid shows a strong self-supporting trump suit with (given a fair break) no losers, as good as six to the four top honours or seven to the three top honours. It is not a stop bid, but may enable partner to go on to a slam holding with virtually no trump support for opener, who has announced that his suit will stand up on its own.	♠ 7 ♥ A 6 ♦ A K Q 9 8 6 5 ♣ 9 6 2

TABLE 21

Opener's Rebid after Direct Raise (Limit-bid)

Bidding	Examples	Comments
		See Table 7 for responder's values.
1♥ – 2♥ No	♠ A 9 3 ♥ K Q J 7 6 ♦ K 4 2 ♣ J 8	On a modest opening hand with no game ambitions facing the single raise, opener should pass. If, however, he elects to bid 3♥ in a competitive auction, for example, over 2♠ or 3♣ bid by his right-hand opponent, this would not be encouraging to responder to advance to game.
1♥ – 2♥ 4♥	♠ A J 10 ♥ A K J 9 7 6 ♦ K J 7 ♣ 9	On a better quality hand opener should bid game direct without putting the onus on responder, or giving away anything to the opponents by taking time to investigate.
1♥ – 2♥ 3♥	♠ 7 3 ♥ A Q 9 8 6 4 ♦ K 8 4 ♣ 9 2	On a weak opening hand with a 6-card suit, a bid of 3♥ by opener may be used pre-emptively, to block a reopening bid by the opposition.
1♥ – 2♥ 2NT	♠ K J 5 ♥ A Q 10 6 ♦ K J 9 ♣ Q J 9	Shows a hand of 17-18 points with a 4-card trump suit. Responder may pass on a weak balanced hand, convert to 3♥ on a minimum or an unbalanced hand unsuitable for play in no-trumps, or raise to 3NT or 4♥ according to his shape and values.

TABLE 21 *(continued)*   53

Bidding	Examples	Comments
1♥ – 2♥ 3♦	♠ A J ♥ A Q J 10 7 ♦ 9 7 4 ♣ K Q 10	If opener is doubtful whether or not to bid game he may make a *trial bid* which, as the two-level raise was not passed, shows better than a minimum opening. A trial bid is usually made in the suit in which help is needed if a game contract is to be undertaken, so here opener bids 3♦. Responder should sign off at the three-level if minimum for his raise, bid game direct if maximum or, if himself doubtful, let his holding in the trial bid suit decide. A shortage (doubleton or singleton) or an honour holding such as ace, king, or queen covered should be considered 'help' (knaves are not helpful on their own but are likely to be in the company of other honours).
1♥ – 2♥ 2♠	♠ K J 9 3 ♥ A Q J 10 7 ♦ 8 ♣ A J 8	Opener's 2♠ is also a *trial bid* (or 3♥ would be in the sequence 1♠-2♠-3♥), but when the suit so trial bid is the second major, it may be a four-card suit. If proposing to give an encouraging reply instead of signing off, responder may raise the second major on 4-card support. Thus it is sometimes possible to find the 4-4 fit and to use opener's original longer suit for discards.

Bidding	Examples	Comments
1♦ – 2♦ 2♥	♠ 7 ♥ A 9 7 ♦ K Q J 9 7 5 ♣ A 6 3	*Trial bids* in the minors differ somewhat, being used to explore for a possible 3NT contract when five of a minor seems out of reach. Here the 2♦ response is likely to include the ♦A and the trial bid of 2♥ shows a stop. If responder's original raise includes a spade stop he will bid 2♠, after which it is reasonable to hope that 3NT can be made. Lacking a spade stop but with a club stop, responder would bid 3♣ and now opener would have to settle for a diamond contract.
1♥ – 3♥ No	♠ A 8 5 ♥ Q 10 9 8 6 3 ♦ 7 2 ♣ K 5	Having opened on a rock-bottom light hand, opener may pass even the strong limit-bid of 3♥. Here he would not have opened at all but for his rebiddable 6-card suit.
1♥ – 3♥ 4♥	♠ A K 5 ♥ Q J 9 8 6 3 ♦ 7 2 ♣ K 5	On this slightly stronger hand opener should accept the invitation and rebid 4♥. Responder will have at least 4-card support which, if not headed by one or both the missing top honours, will contain compensating values outside.
1♠ – 3♠ 4♣	♠ A K J 9 8 ♥ K Q 7 ♦ 8 6 ♣ A Q J	Opener, himself with a strong hand, may initiate slam investigations by a *cue-bid* or, if exceptionally strong, by an immediate 4NT. The cue-bid (now that the suit is agreed and the contract must go at least to game) shows first-round control of the suit bid, and invites responder to cue-

TABLE 21 *(continued)* 55

Bidding	Examples	Comments
		bid his cheapest control in reply. 4♦ would show the ♦A or a void, while ♥ would show the ♥A or a void whilst *denying* the diamond control.
1♣ – 3♣ 3♥	♠ 7 3 ♥ K J 10 ♦ A 6 ♣ A K Q 5 4 3	Opener may judge between passing 3♣, converting to 3NT or, on a good 'shape' hand, bid five of the minor. Here a trial bid could be used, as opener is prepared for any response his partner may make.

Responder's Rebids

Bidding	Comments	Examples
Minimum or sign-off: 1♥ – 1♠ 1NT – 2♠	Opener's rebid being a limit-bid, it demands no further response other than a decision as to the best final contract. Any second-round bid by responder, therefore, is his final decision. Responder would also rebid 2♠ in the sequence 1♥-1♠-2♥ (or 3♠ after 1♥-1♠-2NT).	♠ Q 9 8 7 5 4 ♥ 7 ♦ K 8 3 ♣ 9 4 2
1♥ – 1♠ 2♦ – 2♠ 2NT – 3♠	A series of rebids in responder's suit, all at the lowest available level despite all further efforts by opener, is a sign-off to be respected.	♠ Q 9 8 7 5 4 ♥ 7 ♦ K 8 3 ♣ 9 4 2
1♥ – 1♠ 2♦ – 2♥	Responder's 2♥ rebid is a mere *preference* bid and not a raise of opener's hearts. All responder's points are in black suits, and therefore of little use. As compared with this, a genuine raise would be shown by a jump to 3♥.	♠ K J 9 6 ♥ 10 8 4 ♦ 10 9 ♣ K 7 6 2
1♦ – 1♠ 2♦ – 2♥	A moderate hand, with little or no diamond fit, unable to bid in no-trumps, and anxious to find a better fit somewhere. Clearly a two-suiter lacking power to bid more strongly.	♠ K J 8 7 6 ♥ K J 8 5 3 ♦ 8 ♣ 6 2

TABLE 22 *(continued)* 57

Bidding	Comments	Examples
Stronger hands: 1♦ – 1♥ 2♦ – 2♠	A *responder's reverse* is a one-round force. The second bid suit should not be raised on less than 4-card support, for which reason it can conveniently be used as an	♠ A K 8 ♥ K J 9 7 6 ♦ J 9 7 ♣ J 6
1♥ – 1♠ 2♥ – 3♣	attempt to reach a no-trump game contract. Similarly responder's new suit bid at the three-level is also a one-round force. The same strictures apply and opener should rebid 3NT if he can.	♠ K J 9 7 6 ♥ Q 7 ♦ J 10 6 ♣ A Q J
1♥ – 1♠ 2♣ – 3♠	Responder's jump rebid in his own suit is a strong though non-forcing limit-bid which may be passed by opener on a complete minimum and no fit. In view of the quality of the spade suit, it would be better to bid a fourth suit forcing 2♦ before the 3♠, offering 3NT or 4♠.	♠ A Q J 9 8 7 ♥ 10 2 ♦ K 10 4 ♣ Q 8
1♥ – 1♠ 2♣ – 3♥	A raise as compared with a mere preference, denying the values for an initial 3♥ response (i.e. less than four hearts) or the values for a delayed game raise.	♠ A Q J 8 5 ♥ K J 7 ♦ 9 8 2 ♣ Q 7
1♥ – 1♠ 2♥ – 4♥ or 1♥ – 1♠ 2♣ – 4♥	A *delayed game raise*, showing a supporting hand too good for a 3♥ limit-bid or a direct 4♥ which might mean a missed slam. Responder's 1♠ is a waiting bid which allows him to hear opener's rebid before making his own game bid.	♠ A Q J 7 ♥ K 10 7 5 ♦ K J 8 ♣ 9 2

Bidding	*Comments*	*Examples*
1♥ – 1♠ 2♣ – 2NT	Responder's 2NT rebid still shows 10-12 points, though the chance was taken to show a biddable spade suit first. Responder shows a diamond stop, and a hand worth another try.	♠ A Q J 87 ♥ 10 8 6 ♦ K J 10 ♣ 9 8
Strong hands: 1♥ – 1♠ 2NT – 3♥	Responder's return to opener's original suit at the three-level after the 2NT rebid is *forcing*, giving opener the choice between bidding 3NT or game in his suit, for which responder has better than 3-card support. (Had responder held 4-card trump support, he would have made a limit-bid or used a delayed game raise sequence.)	♠ A K J 9 ♥ Q 10 9 ♦ 9 3 ♣ K 10 8 4
1♥ – 1♠ 2♣ – 2♦	If responder held a diamond stop he could rebid in no-trumps. His 2♦ bid is *fourth suit forcing convention* not *telling*, but *asking* partner to describe his hand further. Opener should give preference to a rebid (if possible) in no-trumps. At the two-level a fourth suit bid is forcing for one round only.	♠ A K J 9 4 ♥ 10 8 ♦ J 9 8 ♣ A Q 9
1♠ – 2♦ 2♥ – 3♣	Used at the three-level, the fourth suit bid promises at least one further bid which means, in practice, that the best game contract, suit or no-trumps, will be reached.	♠ 8 7 5 ♥ Q 9 4 ♦ A K J 9 6 ♣ K 6

TABLE 22 *(continued)* 59

Bidding	Comments	Examples
1♥ – 1♠ 2♣ – 3♦	A jump bid in the fourth suit is unconditionally forcing to game and may conveniently be used in conjunction with the simpler sequences to show slam ambitions with opener's *second* suit agreed as trumps.	♠ K Q 10 8 5 ♥ A 9 3 ♦ 7 ♣ A Q 10 9
1♥ – 1♠ 2♥ – 4♣	A jump bid in a new suit, even though deferred until the second round, is still unconditionally game-forcing. Here, as it by-passes the 3NT level, it requires opener to bid the best suit game contract in the light of his knowledge of responder's obvious two-suiter.	♠ K Q 10 9 7 ♥ 9 8 ♦ 6 ♣ A Q J 9 8

TABLE 23

Two No-trump Opening Bids and Direct Raises

Opener	Responder	Opener's Rebids	Comments
20-22 points in a balanced hand at any score	Raise to 3NT on 4-10 points		Direct raises in no-trumps are judged by responder allowing, between the two hands, 25-26 points for a game, 33-34 points for a small slam, and 37 or more points for a grand slam.
	Raise to 4NT on 11-12 points	Bid 6NT on 22 points	Direct raises are quantitative, highly invitational and based on a known combined minimum of 31 points. Opener should bid 6NT on a 22-point maximum or if he has a strong feature such as a 5-card suit.
	Raise to 6NT on 13-14 points		Opener should pass this direct raise to 6NT as it will only be made in the knowledge that the combined count cannot reach the grand slam zone of 37 or more points.
	Bid 5NT on 15-16 points	Bid 6NT on 20-21 points, or 7NT on 22 points	As 5NT from responder has no natural meaning, it is used as a *demand* to opener to bid 6NT, and an *invitation* to bid the grand slam on an original maximum of 22 points.

TABLE 23 *(continued)* 61

Note: Responder's counts are arbitrary, and due weight must always be given to distribution and the quality of the hand including 'fillers' and suit length. A 4-card suit headed by K-Q, for example, can be counted as 5 points, whereas with a fifth card it is likely to be much more valuable.

Examples:

♠ A K 7 ♥ A Q 9 ♦ K Q 8 7 ♣ K J 8	This is a maximum hand for a 2NT opening so even missing one of the queens it would qualify. Note that vulnerability makes no difference, and ideally all suits should be well guarded.
♠ A Q ♥ A Q 9 ♦ K 10 9 ♣ A Q 10 9 7	Although technically an evenly-balanced hand is called for, many hands which qualify for a 2NT opening also contain a 5-card suit. A good opening here, as it ensures the lead coming up to, and not through the hand.
♠ J 10 6 ♥ K 8 7 4 ♦ 9 5 3 ♣ 10 7 5	Raise an opening 2NT to 3NT. Increase it to 11 points by adding the ♥J and ♦A-Q, and it would become worth a quantitative and invitational bid of 4NT. Strengthen it still further by including the ♣K and the best response is a direct raise to 6NT.
♠ J 10 6 ♥ K J 8 7 ♦ A Q 3 ♣ K J 10	Lastly include the ♣J, making it like this, 15 points with two tens and the response should be 5NT, *demanding* 6NT and *inviting* 7NT. It goes without saying that, should responder's count warrant it, he may bid a direct 7NT himself.

TABLE 24

Suit Responses to Two No-trump Openings

Response	Requirements	Comments
3♣ over 2NT (Baron)*	Unbalanced hand – suit fit seems desirable	A *conventional response* used to investigate for a possible suit fit. It requires opener to bid his 4-card suits in *ascending* order and, if his only 4-card suit is clubs, to rebid 3NT.
3♦ over 2NT	Very weak long suit	*Flint convention* – see Table 25.
3♥ or 3♠	10+ points with long suit	Forcing to game and a mild slam invitation. Opener's rebid of 4NT would be conventional and non-quantitative.
Direct 4♥ or 4♠	4+ points with long suit	A sign-off, which opener should pass.
Direct 4♣	Any strong suit, slam possible	*Gerber convention*, requesting immediate ace-showing from opener. Responses on step principle: 4♦ = 0 or 4 aces, 4♥ = 1 ace, 4♠ = 2 aces, 4NT = 3 aces. As it is most unlikely that opener has no ace at all, in practice this leaves a subsequent bid of 5♣ to ask for kings on the same scale.

* Many players prefer to use straight Stayman (see Table 14) which is perfectly correct and satisfactory except that it does not help towards finding a fit for a minor suit slam.

TABLE 24 *(continued)* 63

Examples:

Opener:	Responder:	Bidding:

♠ A K 9 2   ♠ Q 8 6 3   2NT – 3♣
♥ A Q 6   ♥ J 7 5 3 2   3♦ – 3♥
♦ A J 9 2   ♦ 8 6   3♠ – 4♠
♣ K 9   ♣ J 4

3♣ is forcing at least to game and gives the maximum bidding space for investigations for the best suit fit. Showing suits in ascending order, opener rebids 3♦ and the 4-4 spade fit is discovered quite simply.

♠ A Q 6   ♠ K 5 2   2NT – 3♣
♥ A Q 8   ♥ 6   3NT – 4♣
♦ K Q 9   ♦ A 8 7 6   4NT* – 5♥
♣ K Q 4 3   ♣ A J 10 6 5 5NT – 6♦
                           7♣

* 'Blackwood'

This method is particularly efficient when responder has a possible minor suit slam in view. Opener's 3NT shows that his *only* 4-card suit is clubs, responder's 4♣ is at least a game force in clubs and the grand slam is reached without difficulty.

♠ A 10 9   ♠ 7   2NT – 3♣
♥ A Q 6   ♥ K 9 8 3   3NT – 5♣
♦ A K Q   ♦ 8 6 3 2
♣ K 7 5 4   ♣ Q 10 9 8

Note the direct jump to 5♣ when opener shows that he has no other 4-card suit. Responder prefers the club game contract but has no interest in slam investigations.

Opener:	*Responder:*	*Bidding:*

♠ A 10 9 ♠ 7 2NT – 3♣ With two 4-card suits
♥ A Q 6 4 ♥ K 9 8 3 2 3♥ – 4♥ opener rebids 3♥. He
♦ A K ♦ 8 6 3 could show clubs later
♣ K 7 5 4 ♣ Q 10 9 8 if expedient, but when
responder just raises to
4♥, it is clear that the
best spot has been found

♠ Q J 10 9 6 4 3 2 There is no immediate weak take-out of a
♥ 9 2NT opening bid (but see Flint, Table 25).
♦ 7 3 Bid 3♠ over 2NT and, if opener rebids 3NT,
♣ 8 4 take out into 4♠. In fact, go on repeating
spades at the lowest available level until
partner gets the idea! The 3♠ bid is game-
forcing anyway.

♠ Q J 10 9 6 4 3 2 The addition of the ♦A makes this hand
♥ 9 good enough for a direct 4♠, a *mild slam*
♦ A 7 *invitation* on a hand which *must* be played
♣ 8 4 in spades. If opener rebids 4NT, this would
be conventional and not quantitative and
would be the start of slam investigations
with spades agreed as trumps.

♠ 7 Facing partner's 2NT opening bid, the three
♥ A missing aces are of vital importance. If
♦ K Q J 10 9 7 6 5 opener has them nothing can go amiss with
♣ 8 4 3 a final contract of 7NT (or 7♦ at rubber for
the honours). Bid a direct Gerber 4♣ and if
the response is 4♠ (two aces) bid 6NT to
allow the lead to come up to and not
through his hand. If he bids 4NT to show all
three aces, bid the grand slam.

TABLE 25   65

Flint 3♦ Transfer Convention (Simple)

Requirements	Comments
Facing 2NT opening, long weak major suit in very weak hand with no game ambitions	Flint is the nearest approach to a weak take-out of a 2NT opening, enabling the partnership to play no higher than 3♥ or 3♠. A response of 3♦ (or in the sequence 2♣-2♦-2NT-3♦) requests opener to *transfer* to 3♥. With long hearts responder will then pass or, with long spades, will in turn transfer to 3♠ which opener will also pass.

A genuine strong 3♦ response to the opening 2NT is shown by a responder's *rebid* of 3NT, i.e. 2NT-3♦-3♥-3NT. |

Examples:	
♠ 5 2 ♥ 9 8 7 5 4 3 ♦ 7 6 4 2 ♣ 6	A worthless hand unless played in hearts at the lowest available level. As 3♥ would be forcing to game (see Table 24) bid 3♦ requesting opener to transfer to 3♥, which you will pass.
♠ 9 8 7 5 4 3 ♥ 5 2 ♦ 7 6 4 2 ♣ 6	The same hand with the major suits exchanged. Still a worthless hand unless played in spades. Bid 3♦ which opener will transfer to 3♥. Transfer this to 3♠, which he will also pass.
♠ K 7 ♥ 10 8 5 ♦ Q J 10 8 7 ♣ A Q 6	This responding hand is clearly in the slam zone. Bid 3♦ in response to the 2NT opening and, when opener makes the requested transfer to 3♥, rebid 3NT, which shows a diamond suit in a hand with slam ambitions. On a minimum 20 points and no particular diamond fit, opener would pass. Alternatively he can agree diamonds by bidding 4NT (conventional, not quantitative) or make a cue-

bid. It follows, of course, that with greater strength responder must not risk this sequence and the possible pass of 3NT. Alternatives might be an immediate quantitative 4NT or a Gerber 4♣.

Note: The above is simple Flint. The full version is set out in Table 26.

TABLE 26 67

Flint 3♦ Convention – Optional Extensions

Bidding	Examples	Comments
2NT – 3♦ 3♥ – 3♠ 4♠	♠ A K 9 8 ♥ A J 6 ♦ K 9 ♣ A K 7 4	If responder, as expected when he bids 3♦, holds a long weak heart suit, opener is willing to let him play at the three-level. However, when 3♥ is converted to 3♠, opener, with a maximum, raises to 4♠.
2NT – 3♦ 3♠	♠ K 9 ♥ A K 9 8 ♦ A J 6 ♣ A K 7 4	The same maximum hand with suits exchanged. If opener transfers to 3♥ as requested, responder is likely to pass or himself transfer to 3♠. If responder has long *hearts*, opener sees a play for game so bids 3♠ which responder can pass or convert to 4♥.
2NT – 3♦ 3NT	♠ A K 9 8 ♥ A K 7 4 ♦ A J 6 ♣ K 9	With a magnificent fit for both majors in a maximum hand opener forces the issue by a rebid of 3NT instead of the requested 3♥. Responder must now convert to 4♥ or 4♠, whichever his suit is.

Summary: With a maximum 2NT opening bid containing:
  1 A strong 4-card spade fit, transfer to 3♥.
  2 A strong 4-card heart fit, transfer to 3♠.
  3 Two strong 4-card majors, bid 3NT.

Still further extensions make it possible to stop in a minor suit contract at the four-level:

2NT – 3♦　or　2NT – 3♦ 3♥ – 4♦　　　　3♥ – 4♣	The four-level minor suit bid, whether opener has himself rebid 3♥, 3♠ or 3NT over 3♦, should be passed.
2NT – 3♦　or　2NT – 3♦ 3♥ – 3NT　　　3♥ – 4♦ 　　　　　　　or 4♣	Note the difference between these two sequences. The first shows a responding hand with a genuine diamond suit and mild slam ambitions and the second a weak hand suitable only for the lowest available minor-suit contract.
2♣ – 2♦ 2NT – 3♦ ?	All the Flint conventional sequences may be used when the opening bid and rebid have been 2♣ and 2NT, allowance being made by responder for the greater strength held in a 2♣ opener (see Table 27).

TABLE 27   69

Two Club Opening Bids and Opener's Rebids

Bidding	Examples	Comments – Opener's Rebids
		AN OPENING 2♣ IS UNCONDITIONALLY FORCING TO GAME UNLESS FOLLOWED BY AN OPENER'S REBID OF 2NT. The negative response is 2♦ (see Table 28).
2♣ – 2♦ 2NT	♠ A K 9 ♥ A Q J 6 ♦ A J 7 ♣ K Q 5	23-24 points in a no-trump type hand. The only opener's rebid which may be passed by responder. Responder rebids as set out in Tables 23, 24, 25 (and 26 if desired) except that opener's greater strength must be considered.
2♣ – 2♦ 3NT	♠ A K Q ♥ A Q J 6 ♦ A J 7 ♣ K Q 5	25 or more points in a no-trump type hand. As the rebid is already at game level responder may pass or take further action, such as taking out into a suit contract, if this seems best.
2♣ – 2♦ 2♥	♠ K Q 10 9 ♥ A K J 10 7 ♦ A K 10 ♣ 6	A powerful game-going hand with 9 playing tricks. The suit rebid is *unconditionally game-forcing* and responder must keep the bidding open, if necessary by using the second negative bid of 2NT.

Bidding	Examples	Comments – Opener's Rebids
2♣ – 2♦ 3♣	♠ 8 ♥ K 8 ♦ A K 10 ♣ A K Q 9 8 7 6	When the predominating suit is clubs, the opening values may be devalued slightly, but the 3♣ rebid is still forcing to game.

Note: Count points *only* when a rebid in no-trumps is to be made. For a 2♣ opening with a suit rebid the requirements are *nine playing tricks* in a powerful game-going hand needing the minimum of support.

Bidding	Examples	Comments
2♣ – 2♦ 3♥ or 3♠ – ?	♠ A K Q ♥ K Q J 10 6 5 ♦ A K Q ♣ 6	Opener's jump suit rebid is *a conventional demand* to responder to cue-bid any ace he may hold in spite of his 2♦ negative. If responder has the ♥A *or* ♣A, opener will bid 6♥. Missing both, which responder shows by a forced rebid of 3NT, opener converts to 4♥. Responder cannot hold two aces or he would have had a positive response instead of a negative.
2♣ – 2♦ 3♥ – 3NT No	♠ A K Q ♥ K Q J ♦ A K Q ♣ K Q J 9	If two aces are missing, opener can also elect to pass the 3NT response. Thus on this rare type of hand a bidding level may be saved by replacing the usual 4NT request for aces by this jump suit rebid. (Compare also the Acol opening 4NT and the Acol direct king convention, Table 42.)

TABLE 28　　　　　71

Responses to Two Club Openings – Negative and Rebids

Bidding	Examples	Comments
		Facing a 2♣ opening bid responder bids 2♦, a negative response, to deny a holding as good as: 1　Any one ace and king 2　Any 8 points which include one king Responder's second negative, if he is compelled to rebid, is 2NT.
2♣ – 2♦ 2NT – No or 2♣ – 2♦ 2♠ – 2NT	♠9 8 5 ♥8 7 4 3 ♦J 10 7 ♣8 6 4	Responder may pass opener's 2NT rebid which shows 23-24 points. If opener rebids 2♠, responder must rebid, and uses the second negative of 2NT. Had opener's rebid been 2♥, responder bids 3♥.
2♣ – 2♦ 2♥ – 2♠	♠K J 10 7 5 ♥7 2 ♦6 4 2 ♣9 7 6	Once having denied positive values with 2♦, responder may bid constructively if possible. He may show a biddable suit, raise responder's suit on 4-card support or three to an honour, or raise a 2NT rebid to 3NT on 3 points or even a 5-card suit headed by a queen. Either Baron or Flint may be used (Tables 24 & 25).

Bidding	Examples	Comments
2♣ – 2♦ 2♥ – 4♥	♠ Q 10 7 ♥ K 8 7 4 ♦ J 9 ♣ J 10 8 5	Raise to the 4-level on 4-card trump support and about 6-7 honour points (cf. the double raise of an opening strong two, Table 31). This bid also denies any first-round control.
2♣ – 2♦ 2♥ – 3♠	♠ K Q J 10 8 5 ♥ 8 ♦ 9 4 ♣ J 9 8 6	A JUMP RESPONDER'S REBID FOLLOWING HIS 2♦ negative IS CONVENTIONAL, showing a solid trump suit *missing the ace*. Note that had the suit been headed by the ace, the hand would have been worth an original positive response.
2♣ – 2♦ 3♥ – 4♦	♠ 9 8 5 ♥ 8 6 4 ♦ A 7 6 ♣ 8 7 4 3	THE JUMP SUIT REBID BY OPENER IS CONVENTIONAL (see Table 27). It requires responder to cue-bid any ace held in spite of the 2♦ negative. So here responder cue-bids the ♦A. With no ace he is required to rebid 3NT. Note that he cannot have two aces or he would have had an original positive response.

TABLE 29　　　　　　73

Positive Responses to Two Club Openings

Bidding	Examples	Comments
		The requirements for a positive response (see Table 28) may be slightly relaxed if it is clear that this will not cost bidding space. Thus a two-level response (2♥ or 2♠) can be made on slightly less than the necessary 8 points. A positive response in diamonds must be 3♦, as 2♦ would be negative.
2♣ – 2♠	♠ A J 8 7 6 ♥ 10 9 5 4 ♦ Q 8 6 ♣ 7	Slightly under strength for a positive response but 2♠ now is likely to be far more helpful and constructive than 2♦ and then a spade rebid.
2♣ – 2♠	♠ A J 8 7 ♥ K 5 4 ♦ 10 6 2 ♣ 5 4 3	8 points and a biddable suit, qualifying the hand for a positive response. Exchange the suits, making the spades into diamonds, and there is insufficient strength to raise the level by bidding 3♦, so make a positive response of 2NT.
2♣ – 3♦	♠ A 9 3 ♥ 5 4 3 ♦ K J 10 7 6 ♣ 6 2	Worth a positive response of 3♦ (not 2♦ which would be negative). Make the ♦6 into another small club, and the original positive response should be 2NT.

Bidding	Examples	Comments
2♣ – 2NT	♠ K J 7 ♥ Q 10 8 ♦ Q J 9 6 ♣ 10 9 6	A positive response of 2NT. Increase the strength by making the two queens into kings and the response should be 3NT – a bid to be avoided if possible as it uses bidding space which might be better employed for exploration.
2♣ – 2♦ 2NT – 3♣ ?	♠ J 9 7 6 ♥ J 7 6 3 ♦ 10 ♣ A Q 10 4	Not worth a positive response of 3♣ and neither majors is biddable at this stage. Bid 2♦ and if opener rebids 2NT rebid 3♣ to investigate for a suit fit (see Table 24). If the clubs were either hearts or spades the hand would be worth the two-level positive response.
2♣ – 3♥	♠ 8 3 ♥ A K Q 9 8 5 4 ♦ 8 5 3 ♣ 4	AN IMMEDIATE JUMP RESPONSE IN A SUIT IS CONVENTIONAL, SHOWING A SOLID AND SELF-SUPPORTING TRUMP SUIT AS GOOD AS SIX TO THE FOUR TOP HONOURS OR SEVEN TO THE A-K-Q. This response may enable opener to bid a slam in partner's suit even if this is his own short suit.

TABLE 30   75

Strong Two Opening Bids and Opener's Rebids

The Acol strong two opening bids (in spades, hearts, or diamonds) are *not* glorified one-bids. Of no specific point count, though usually in the mid- to high teens, they show hands of character on which opener can afford to skip one level of bidding to show playing strength, to ensure himself a rebid, and to allow responder to judge the worth of even meagre supporting values.

Strong twos are *forcing for one round* with a responder's negative of 2NT (see Table 31). They are *game-forcing* in three situations:
1   Following opener's jump rebid in a new suit.
2   Following opener's reverse rebid.
3   Following any first-round positive response.

Strong twos fall into three classes:
1   Hands containing 8 playing tricks based on one long strong suit.
2   Highly distributional two-suiters which are likely to produce game if the best fit is found – hence opener's need to ensure a rebid to show his second suit.
3   Strong distributional hands with high point count though lacking the 9 playing tricks needed for a 2♣ opening (see Table 27). This is the type most frequently missed, as it may appear to fall between the upper limits of a one-bid and the lower limits of a strong two. The deciding factor will be the need to ensure a rebid as well as to make responder aware of the potential strength of the hand.

Examples:

♠ 8
♥ A K Q J 7 6 4
♦ A 5
♣ 7 5 3

When calculating playing tricks you are entitled to assume a reasonable division of the outstanding cards, so here it is fair to count seven playing tricks in hearts plus the ♦A. Open 2♥ and rebid a simple 3♥.

♠ A K Q J 6 4
♥ 9 3
♦ A K
♣ J 10 3

It is fair to count the solid 6-card spade suit as worth six playing tricks which, plus the ♦ A-K, make eight. Open 2♠ and rebid 3♠ over any response. If responder bid 2NT originally, he may now pass.

♠ A K Q J 6 4 3
♥ 9
♦ A K
♣ J 10 3

Open 2♠ and if responder bids 2NT rebid 4♠. It is worth trying for game even in the face of a negative response – as little as the ♣Q in responder's hand would allow you to develop ten tricks.

♠ K Q 8
♥ A K J 10 7 4 3
♦ K 5
♣ 3

Open 2♥ so that responder will know how little help you need to make this hand worth a game contract. If he holds as little as three small hearts and one ace he would pass a 1♥ opening with 4♥ almost a certainty.

♠ A Q J 8 5 3
♥ A J 10 7 6 4
♦ 6
♣ –

A strong two-suiter on which it is vitally important to ensure the opportunity to show both suits, so as to play in the best available fit. Open 2♠ and over a 2NT response bid 3♥, not forcing, so responder may pass, give preference to 3♠ or, knowing the strength and character of opener's hand, raise to the four-level in the better-fitting.

TABLE 30 (continued) 77

♠ 7 ♥ A K Q 7 5 3 ♦ – ♣ A Q J 9 7 5	Wanting to play in game at all costs, open 2♥ and over a 2NT response bid 4♣, game-forcing. Responder must convert to 4♥ or raise to 5♣. Exchange the suits making it a spade-heart two-suiter and you should open 2♠ and rebid 4♥ (asking merely for preference) over a 2NT response.
♠ A K Q 10 8 ♥ A Q J 10 7 3 ♦ 5 ♣ 2	Here again you want to play in game but have no need to conceal that your heart suit is the longer. Open 2♥ and over 2NT reverse (forcing) into 3♠, allowing partner to convert to 4♥ or raise to 4♠.
♠ A K 9 ♥ K J 10 7 6 5 ♦ A K 8 ♣ 7	Not quite qualifying for a 2♣ opening (see Table 27) and too good to risk a one-level bid which might be passed when even the ♥Q-x and either ♠Q or ♦Q would produce a game. Open 2♥ and rebid 3♥ over a 2NT negative.
♠ A K J 10 7 ♥ A Q 10 4 ♦ K Q 8 ♣ 7	Responder might easily pass a 1♠ opening when a heart game is 'cold'. Remember that when one hand is exceptionally strong there is always a risk that responder will not be good enough to bid freely – or to realise how much even 3 or 4 points may be worth. Open 2♠ and rebid 3♥ on the next round.
♠ 10 9 ♥ A K 9 8 6 ♦ A Q J 10 7 ♣ 6	*Not* a hand on which to insist on a high-level contract if partner cannot respond freely and, therefore, not qualifying for an opening strong two. Open 1♥ and await developments – you can always force with 3♦ on the second round if responder bids freely.

TABLE 31

Responses to Strong Two Opening Bids

Response	Requirements	Comments
2NT on weakness (2♥ – 2NT)	Weak hand not qualifying for a positive response	A STRONG TWO OPENING BID IS FORCING FOR ONE ROUND, the negative being 2NT. Positive holdings are set out below – any one of which makes the sequence forcing to game, but even a negative hand may be worth a subsequent game bid.
Example: ♠ 8 ♥ J 8 6 5 ♦ 10 9 8 6 4 ♣ 8 5 4		Respond 2NT to any opening strong two as opener may have game 'cold' in his own hand, which he can then bid direct. He might also have a two-suiter based on spades and a red suit. Raise his rebid of 3♥ or 3♦ to four.
Take-out into new suit at the two-level (2♥ – 2♠)	A biddable suit plus at least one honour trick	If a positive response is possible it is generally best to give preference to trump agreement if held. There is, therefore, a negative inference to be drawn from the fact that a change-of-suit response was preferred.
Take-out into new suit at the three-level (2♥ – 3♦)	5-card suit and better honour content (1½ honour tricks)	As in responding to a one-bid, greater strength is required if the bidding level must be raised. As opener will always rebid himself, there is time for responder to go quietly, knowing that he too will have a chance to rebid.

TABLE 31 (continued)   79

Examples:

♠ Q 9 7
♥ A J 9 6
♦ 8 4
♣ J 8 7 5

If opener bids 2♦ respond 2♥. If he opens 2♥ respond 3♥. If he opens 2♠ respond 3♠ (see below). Exchange the *red* suits and, if opener bids 2♥ it is best to respond 2NT before subsequently making sure a game is reached.

♠ Q 9
♥ A J 9 6 3
♦ 8 4
♣ J 8 7 5

If opener bids 2♠ respond 3♥ (or 2♥ over an opening 2♦). But exchange the ♥3 for the ♦3, and the initial response to 2♠ should be 2NT. If opener rebids 3♠ raise to 4♠ as ♠Q-x is adequate support for an opening two-bid.

Response	Requirements	Comments
Single raise in opener's suit (2♥ – 3♥)	Trump support and *at least one ace or void*	An unlimited response, possibly on a minimum but it may be a prelude to slam investigations. A suit worth a strong two opening does not need 4-card support and immediate trump support, if available, is most likely to facilitate the rest of the auction.
Double raise in opener's suit (2♥ – 4♥)	Good trump suport, about 10 honour points, and *no ace or void*	Not a shut-out bid but, being immediate denial of any first-round control, opener must provide at least three of these himself if contemplating a slam try. Opener's rebid of 4NT would be the *Acol direct king convention* (see Table 42).
Direct 3NT (2♥ – 3NT)	10-12 points in evenly-balanced *aceless* hand	Denies any first-round control, either ace or void. Also, by inference, denies three-card trump support for suit opened, or a direct suit raise would have been preferred.

Response	Requirements	Comments
Jump take-out in a new suit (2♠ – 4♥)	A solid and self-supporting trump suit	A conventional response showing a solid suit as good as six to the four top honours or seven to the A-K-Q. It also, by inference, denies support for opener's suit (see below).

Examples:

♠ 6 5 4 3
♥ K 10 9
♦ A 7 5 4
♣ 10 9

If opener bids 2♣, 2♥ or 2♦, raise to three of that suit, confirming adequate support for a suit opened at the two-level and at least one ace or void (i.e. one first-round control).

♠ K 9 8 2
♥ –
♦ A K Q 9 8 7 5
♣ 6 4

If opener bids 2♥ bid 4♦ (see above). If he opens 2♠, however, knowing that this will be the final denomination, raise to 3♠ rather than show the diamond side-suit. If opener merely raises 3♠ to 4♠ you will have to be the one to make a slam-try (cue-bid 5♦). But if over the 3♠ he cue-bids the club ace (4♣) bid 5NT (grand slam force, see Table 10).

♠ Q J 9 4
♥ K 7 6 5
♦ K 8 7 4
♣ 8

If opener bids 2♦, 2♥ or 2♠, raise to four of that suit showing good trump support but no ace or void. Note the jump to 4♦, not to game, which leaves the 4NT level available if opener wants to ask for kings (Acol direct king convention, Table 42).

♠ Q J 9
♥ K Q J 9 6
♦ K 8 7 4
♣ 8

♠ Q-J-9 is very adequate support for a 2♠ opening, which raise to 4♠ in preference to bidding 3♥. Similarly, facing a 2♦ opening, a raise to 4♦ is likely to be more constructive than a change-of-suit 2♥ which does *not* immediately deny an ace or void.

TABLE 31 *(continued)*   81

♠ J 7 ♥ K J 9 2 ♦ K 10 8 3 ♣ Q J 10	If opener bids 2♦ or 2♥, raise to four of that suit. If opener bids 2♠ respond 3NT, showing the count and denying any first-round control. Opener's rebid of 4NT would, of course, be the Acol direct king convention.
♠ A K Q J 9 6 ♥ 9 5 ♦ 7 6 ♣ J 8 4	If opener bids 2♦ or 2♥ make the conventional response of 3♠ showing the solid self-supporting suit. The final contract must be at least a game and opener's knowledge that his partner's suit needs no support may greatly facilitate reaching a slam.

Intervening Bids, Simple and Forcing

Objects:	To take the offensive, to direct partner's lead if you become the defenders and to disrupt the opponents' bidding sequences. The risks of intervening and possibly incurring a heavy penalty must, however, be balanced against your possible gains.

Bid	*Comments*
Suit overcall at lowest available level: 1♥ – 1♠ or 1♥ – 2♥	An intervening bid made at the lowest available level should be based on playing tricks rather than honour strength, within two tricks of the bid if vulnerable and three if not vulnerable. Try to make such an intervention in a suit in which you would like to play as declarer or would like your partner to lead if you become defenders.
	Remember that 1♠ over opponent's opening 1♥ uses no bidding space, as a minor suit response would in any case have to be made at the two-level. But to intervene with 1♠ over 1♣ prevents a one-level response in either red suit, or 2♣ over 1♦ prevents a one-level bid in either major.
Examples: ♠ 9 7 ♥ K 8 4 ♦ K Q 9 8 6 3 ♣ A J	Bid 1♦ over an opposing 1♣ or 2♦ over 1♥ or 1♠. Reduce the diamonds to a 5-card suit and intervention, particularly if vulnerable, becomes dangerous. But head the 5-card suit with K-Q-J and it is worth the two-level intervention.

TABLE 32 *(continued)* 83

Bid	Comments
♠ K J 10 7 5 4 ♥ 9 8 6 ♦ A 6 3 ♣ 8	Although containing only 8 honour points, there is good compensating suit length, worth an intervening bid. Compare the hand below, however, which is much stronger in points but has no playing strength and is, therefore, not safe for an intervening bid: ♠ A 10 6 ♥ 9 7 5 ♦ A J 10 ♣ A 9 4 3
Jump overcall, one extra level: 1♥ – 2♠ or 3♦	A strong, highly invitational but non-forcing bid. It must vary according to tactical considerations of score, etc, but should contain a good 6-card suit and about 6½ -7 playing tricks in a single-suited hand unfitted for defence.
♠ A K J 9 8 5 ♥ 7 ♦ A 10 4 ♣ K 10 8	Bid 2♠ over any opening one-bid as the hand is too strong for a simple one-level bid. Exchange the black suits and it would be worth a jump of 3♣ over 1♦, 1♥ or 1♠. Responses to jump overcalls should be based on the fact that partner has at least a 6-card suit (making even a doubleton-honour adequate trump support). Responder should make a bid even if less than the barest values for a reply to an ordinary opening one-bid are held.
♠ A K J 9 8 5 ♥ K Q 8 ♦ A 9 ♣ K 10	Double an opening one-bid and then take-out partner's response into spades, showing an even stronger hand than the one above.
Jump overcall, two or more levels: 1♥ – 3♠ or 4♦	A jump intervening bid of two or more levels, i.e. one or more levels than needed to show a strong hand, is pre-emptive. It announces weakness except in the suit bid and is intended to obstruct the opposition's bidding

Bid	Comments
	sequence to the limit. Tactically a direct jump to game, particularly when partner has passed, may well block an opposition game or slam.
♠ K Q J 9 8 7 5 2 ♥ 9 ♦ 9 7 ♣ 8 4	Bid 3♠ over your right-hand opponent's 1♣, 1♦ or 1♥, even if partner has not passed. This will warn him of the character of the hand. Add an outside ace and it would be worth a jump to 4♠ (indicating not more than two defensive tricks).
Overcall of 1NT	Shows a balanced hand with a minimum of 15-16 points and a stop in the suit opened against you. It is unwise to devalue this bid because of the risk of being 'sandwiched' between the opening bid and values for a business double on your left.
♠ A Q 7 ♥ K J 8 ♦ K J 9 7 ♣ K J 10	Overcall any opening suit by right-hand opponent with 1NT. Partner should respond as he would to an opening strong no-trump. 2♣ is Stayman.
Overcall in opponent's suit: 1♥ – 2♥	This bid is now used as a *game force* showing a powerful hand unsuited to a take-out double (see Table 38). This will be because of the risk that partner might pass for penalties. Responder shows suits in ascending order.
♠ A K 9 8 6 ♥ 6 ♦ A Q J 9 6 ♣ K 7 or	Bid 2♥ over an opening 1♥. Partner will almost inevitably bid 3♣ after which rebid 3♦ which, as you do not pass or support clubs, shows a diamond/spade two-suiter. Increase the strength by including the ♦K and the ♣A

TABLE 32 *(continued)* 85

Bid	Comments
♠ A K 9 8 6 ♥ 6 ♦ A K Q 9 6 ♣ A 7	in place of the ♣K, and the hand would qualify for a game-forcing *repeat* of opponent's suit.
Overcall of 2NT over 1NT	An Acol conventional bid, game-forcing, showing a powerful two-suiter, ensuring the chance to show both suits. It takes the place of a take-out double of a 1NT opening *which is always primarily intended for penalties.*
♠ – ♥ A K J 9 5 3 ♦ A K J 8 7 6 ♣ 6	Bid 2NT over opponent's opening 1NT. Partner will respond as to a take-out double (see Table 39) by showing his best suit.

Unusual No-trump Convention

This convention is widely used and should be understood by any aspiring player. It may be defined as a form of take-out double expressing shape rather than honour strength and is generally used in preparation for a possible sacrifice contract.

Using the *unusual no-trump convention*, any bid in no-trumps when this cannot be understood as natural is a request to partner to take action. When the opponents have bid in two suits, it asks partner to show the better of his two remaining suits. When the opponents have bid in one major suit only, it asks for partner's better minor suit.

Examples:

N	E	S	W	
1♠	–	2♥	2NT	West's 2NT asks for East's choice between clubs and diamonds.
–	?			

1♠	2NT	–	?	This time West's choice between the minors is again requested.

1♠	–	2♦	2NT	Here the requested choice is between the two unbid suits, hearts and clubs.
–	?			

1♠	–	2♥	–	Obviously East refrained from earlier action in the hope that North-South would not bid to game. Now that they have done so he foresees a possibly good sacrifice in clubs or diamonds, whichever fits West's hand best. He might hold something like the example shown when, particularly if not vulnerable against vulnerable opponents, 5♣ or 5♦, even if doubled, would probably pay dividends.
3♥	–	4♠	–	
–	4NT	–	?	

♠ 8 7
♥ –
♦ K J 9 7 6 3
♣ A 9 8 6 5

TABLE 34   87

Defence to Opponent's Opening 1NT

Over 1NT opening:	Examples	Comments
2♥ or 2♠	♠ A Q J 9 8 5 ♥ K 6 ♦ Q 9 3 ♣ 9 6	Two of a major suit natural and to play. Partner may raise if he sees prospects of game in the light of the certain 6-card suit bid over 1NT.
Double	♠ K J 8 ♥ A J 10 9 6 ♦ Q 10 9 ♣ K 8	Intended primarily for penalties. Should contain upper limit of known count of opening 1NT and preferably a reasonable suit in which to attack. Partner will only take out on a hand totally un-suited to defence (possibly too weak) or with a better contract in view.
2NT	♠ A Q J 9 7 6 ♥ A K J 8 6 3 ♦ 7 ♣ –	A powerful two-suiter. A conventional game-force (see Table 32). Partner will respond as to a take-out double, showing his best suit, and will keep the auction open to game.
2♣ or 2♦	♠ K 8 6 4 3 ♥ A 10 9 ♦ K J 7 6 ♣ 7	The Astro defence. 2♣ or 2♦ is conventional, showing a hand not strong enough for, or unsuit-able for, a penalty double. 2♣ shows a minimum of 9 cards between hearts and one of the minors. 2♦ shows 9 cards between spades and one of the other suits. Here, bid 2♦ to show that spades is the anchor major.

In these days of weak no-trump opening bids, it is essential to have a clearly-formulated policy for defensive action. The overcalls on page 87 may be used to counter a strong no-trump also though, of course, with considerable added strength. They are based on a 12-14 point no-trump opening.

Responding to 2♣ or 2♦	With 3 cards in the anchor major and insufficient points for game, bid at the two-level. A jump to three-level shows a 4-card trump fit, and is invitational, not forcing. An immediate raise to game guarantees 4-card support and is natural, intending to play.
	Lacking even three of the anchor major, bid two of the 'neutral' suit – the next one up. Pass if you have a weak hand with a long weak holding in the Astro minor.
	With a good hand and six cards in another suit, jump take-out in the new suit or raise the original Astro bid. This is highly invitational but not forcing. The only forcing bid is 2NT. This suggests a possible game contract without promising a further bid, and also promises some support for the anchor major. Opener should clarify his hand by showing his other suit.

There are numerous conventions for use against an opening 1NT. Variations of Astro include Pin-point Astro, Aspro and Asptro. Whichever you decide to use, make sure that your partner is on the same wavelength!

TABLE 35   89

Protective Bids

When two passes have followed the opening bid, opener's partner is known to be extremely weak. Second-in-hand may have passed because of a good holding in the suit opened or because his hand contains no sensible intervening bid. Fourth hand is now in the *protective* position and may take action as follows:

Bid	Comments	Examples
Simple overcall in new suit	On the assumption that as opener could only bid at the one-level and his partner could not respond at all, second-in-hand is likely to have some values. The weakest protective bid, used to take an opportunity to contest the part-score, is a simple new suit bid, which may be made on as little as 8 points at the one-level (more if at the two-level).	♠ K J 8 7 5 ♥ A 5 4 ♦ 7 6 ♣ J 10 9 Protect a 1♣, 1♦ or 1♥ opening with 1♠
Protective 1NT	This bid may be made on as little as 10-11 points which include a stop in the suit opened. Here bid 1NT if opener's 1♥ is passed round to you.	♠ A 7 6 ♥ Q J 10 ♦ K J 9 3 ♣ 10 9 8
Jump bid in new suit	Shows a good hand with a strong suit of its own, and a genuine wish to contest for game or part-score. Here bid 2♠ if opener's 1♥ is passed round to you.	♠ A Q J 6 4 3 ♥ 5 ♦ K Q 9 ♣ A 6 3

Bid	Comments	Examples
Double	A protective double, which may well be converted to a business double by a pass from partner, who may have been unable to intervene because of his holding in the suit opened, must be based on not less than 11 points and preferably more. Here double a 1♦ opening passed round to you. You will be happy to defend if partner passes and equally, if he takes out because lacking sufficient trumps, he can play safely in any other suit.	♠ K J 10 7 ♥ K J 9 5 ♦ A 7 ♣ J 10 9

Note: The partner of a player who bids in the protective position must bear in mind the low values which may be held by his partner and should bid or raise far less freely than in response to an immediate overcall.

TABLE 36   91

Pre-emptive Opening Bids

The object of a pre-emptive opening bid is to rob the opponents of bidding space. This may prevent them from entering the auction or cause them to reach the wrong contract.

Requirements	*Comments*
One long suit in a weak hand, about 6 playing tricks not vulnerable and 7 if vulnerable for an opening three-bid	Qualifying hands should be worthless in defence, useless in support of partner and, as a corollary to this, containing very little in any unbid major. Hands with two or more honour tricks or with a 4-card holding in a second major are not suitable. Fourth-in-hand opening pre-emptive bids do not exist, as there is no need to obstruct opponents who could not open. First or second in hand pre-emptive bids are excellent, the idea being to strike before the opponents get together, but the best position for an opening pre-emptive bid is third-in-hand after two passes.
Example: ♠ 7 ♥ A Q 8 6 5 4 3 ♦ 9 7 5 ♣ 6 2	Except as fourth-in-hand after three passes (when pass) open 3♥. Any action by opponents will now have to start at a high level which may make it impossible for them to discover their best contract.
Four bids: As above but slightly stronger	In the minor suits an opening four-bid is identical with an opening three except that it should be slightly stronger. Made in hearts or spades, however, an opening four-bid shows a potential game hand containing *not more than two defensive tricks*. Partner must not make a slam try with less than two aces.

Examples: ♠ 7 ♥ K Q J 10 6 4 3 2 ♦ 8 ♣ A 9 3	Open 4♥ (particularly if partner has passed) for which there should be a very good play, apart from being very highly obstructive to opponents with possible spade ambitions. No slam will be made unless partner has two aces and other assistance.
♠ 6 ♥ 3 2 ♦ K 8 ♣ A K J 9 8 4 3 2	Again, particularly if partner has passed, the very high level opening bid of 5♣, which is even more difficult to counter than an opening three-bid, it may well make it impossible for opponents to find their major suit game or slam.
3NT Opening	The gambling 3NT, now an integral part of the Acol system. Should be based on a minimum of a solid 7-card minor with virtually nothing outside.
Example: ♠ 3 2 ♥ 8 5 ♦ Q 7 ♣ A K Q J 9 7 6	The responses are given in Table 44, p.109. Responder, if holding one honour (say ♦Q) knows that opener's minor must be clubs.

TABLE 37   93

Responding to Partner's Pre-emptive Opening Bids

Occasionally as dealer or second-in-hand your partner will open a pre-emptive three-bid before you have had a chance to bid. If you have a strong hand it will, in fact, be you and not the opponents who are in trouble. The following responding bids (some of which are considerably modified from those appearing in the original edition of *Basic Acol*) are given as guidance in this difficult situation. The example hands are based on the correct response to *partner's opening 3♥ bid*.

Requirements and Appropriate Action	Examples
With *moderate supporting values*, pass, hoping that what you have will help partner to come near to making his contract. Knowing the character of his hand, there is no need to bid unless the opposition tries to gain the contract, when further action may be indicated. This is purely a matter of judgement.	♠ A J 9 ♥ 9 7 5 4 ♦ K Q 7 ♣ Q 9 3
With *a strong fit for opener's suit and little else*, make an 'anticipatory' or 'advance' sacrifice of an immediate raise in his suit, which may make it even more difficult for the opponents to discover their own best contract than the original three-bid has done.	♠ 9 2 ♥ K J 8 7 4 2 ♦ 8 ♣ Q 8 7 2
With *three or more honour tricks* and no higher ambitions raise opener's suit to game. As he will have at least a 6-card suit and possibly even more, little trump support will be needed. Your outside values, if they turn out to be well placed, may produce game.	♠ A 10 8 ♥ J 7 ♦ A Q 8 4 ♣ K Q 9 3

Requirements and Appropriate Action	*Examples*
With *a long strong suit and other values* bid game direct, which is not likely to be misunderstood, but never 'rescue' into a new suit which has no guarantee of being better than opener's. Here *don't* bid the spades – pass.	♠ K J 10 8 6 3 ♥ 9 ♦ Q 7 4 ♣ A Q 7
A take-out into a new suit below game-level is a *game force*. In principle, a take-out into a major is a game force and into a minor, a slam try. Here bid 3♠ over 3♥, which opener may raise to 4♠ on even a doubleton. If he rebids 4♥, pass.	♠ A K J 9 8 6 ♥ K 7 3 ♦ K Q 8 ♣ 6
On this second example, bid 4♣ over 3♥, a slam try in *hearts*. It would be dangerous to bid 3♠, which might be raised to 4♠ on only a doubleton.	♠ A Q J 9 ♥ K J 7 ♦ 9 ♣ A K J 7 4
A take-out into 3NT implies either a fit for opener's suit (plus other values) which will enable the long suit to be run *or* a long strong suit (probably a minor) plus outside values, which can be cashed with more chance of taking nine tricks in no-trumps than eleven in a minor suit. Both these hands offer a good chance in no-trumps, the first because of the heart fit and the second because of the long solid club suit.	♠ K Q J 7 ♥ K J 6 ♦ K 9 7 ♣ A Q 7 ♠ K J 10 ♥ 9 ♦ A Q ♣ A K Q J 9 8 6

TABLE 38   95

Countering Pre-emptive Opening Bids

Pre-emptive openings, when used against you, are likely to be obstructive to your bidding as, made by your side, they are to your opponents. There are various ways of countering them between which you can choose as your experience grows. Meanwhile the simplest is *3NT for a take-out* or, alternatively, lower available minor, i.e. 3♦ over 3♣ or 4♣ over any other opening 3-bid.

Requirements and Appropriate Action	*Examples*
With a reasonably good hand *and a long strong suit of your own*, overcall in that suit. But bid to the full limit of the hand, i.e. the lowest available level or direct to game. Here overcall any other opening 3-bid with 3♠. Make the ♣2 into the ♠2, and you should overcall with 4♠.	♠ A K Q 9 7 3 ♥ K J 7 ♦ A J ♣ 7 2
With a *strong hand and damaging holding in the enemy suit*, double. Such a double is intended for penalties, and partner will not take out unless he sees prospects of a better contract. Here double either major suit if opened against you at the three-level.	♠ K J 8 9 6 ♥ A K 10 4 ♦ 9 6 3 ♣ A Q
As the double is reserved for penalties, with *a strong hand short in the suit opened against you*, bid 3NT as a request to partner to take out into his own best suit. He will only pass this, that is, convert it to 3NT to play, with a good stop in the suit opened. As partner's response is forced, don't be too optimistic about his values. Bid 3NT over 3♣ or 3♦ and, if partner bids the other minor, take out into spades.	♠ A Q J 9 6 ♥ A J 10 7 ♦ K 3 ♣ K 2

Requirements and Appropriate Action	Examples
On an extremely strong hand, use a cue-bid of opponent's suit – again, of course, demanding a take-out but leaving no chance that the 3NT take-out request will be passed. Here you don't mind what partner's best suit is as long as he has one! Bid 4♦ over 3♦ opened against you.	♠ A K Q 8 ♥ A Q J 5 ♦ 7 ♣ K Q 10 9

Over opening pre-emptive four bids – even more difficult to counter – the best attempt is to bid 4NT for a take-out over a *major* suit opening and to make an *optional double* over a minor.

When the opening bid has been 4♠, partner will be able to show his own best suit over 4NT, but if the opening has been 4♥, there is a strong inference that the take-out request is based on the minors, as the chance to bid 4♠ was not taken.

4NT for a take-out over the minors uses too much bidding space, as it prevents a final contract of 4♥ or 4♠. A double in this situation shows fair defensive values and partner should stand it unless it is clear that there is a better spot, most notably 4♠ over 4♥.

TABLE 39   97

Take-out Doubles

Definition

A double requests partner to take out into his own best suit when:

1 It is made at the first available opportunity.

2 When the doubler has not missed a previous chance to double the suit bid.

3 The doubler's partner has not bid (other than to pass), has not doubled or made a penalty pass.

A *take-out* (or informatory) *double* of a one- or two-level opening bid is used in preference to a suit or no-trump intervening bid when you want to *ask* partner, rather than tell him, the best spot to play the hand. A minimum of 12 honour points is required and distribution should include:

1 Support for the unbid suits.
2 Shortage in the suit doubled.
3 A good suit with support in a second suit, preferably any unbid major. Note: A take-out double of a major infers a strong interest in the other major.

The doubler should be prepared for any response from partner, including a penalty pass (see Table 39).

Strong unbalanced hands should be shown by a jump bid, a double followed by a transfer to own best suit or by a cue-bid in opponent's suit (Table 32). A double of an opening 1NT is for penalties (Table 33). See also Table 34 on Protection.

Examples:

♠ 5
♥ A Q J 4
♦ K 10 7 2
♣ K 10 8 5

An ideal hand for a take-out double of an opening 1♠, as your partner's longest suit will be the best choice for trumps. You have no way of guessing which this will be, so use the double to *ask* him.

♠ K 10 6 4
♥ A K J 7 2
♦ 9
♣ A 6 5

Double an opening 1♣ or 1♦ in preference to making an intervening bid in hearts. A 4-4 spade fit would be ideal if partner has it – a contract which might well be missed after a suit overcall. If partner, instead of bidding 1♠, bids the other minor, take out into hearts at the lowest available level.

♠ 6 2
♥ Q J 9 6 3
♦ A Q 9
♣ A J 4

Double an opening 1♠ in preference to bidding 2♥ which might be doubled (for a disastrous penalty) by your left-hand opponent. The take-out double gives the best chance of finding the correct resting-place – possibly in two of a minor.

♠ K J 8 7
♥ A Q 8 6
♦ 8 4 2
♣ A 10

NOTE THIS EXCEPTION TO THE RULES ABOVE. If 1♥ or 1♠ is opened against you, you have the distribution but *not the values* for an overcall of 1NT. Double any suit opened against you. If this is a major, and partner responds in your weakness, diamonds, pass. If 1♦ has been opened you cannot let this go uncontested, and *must* ask partner for his choice by doubling.

TABLE 40   99

Responding to a Take-out Double when there has been no Intervening Bid

Holding	Response	Examples
A very weak hand	Show any 4-card suit at the one-level rather than a 5-card suit when this must be bid at the two-level. If this still gives no sensible response, use a *weakness bid of the next higher suit*. The only occasion when this may cause difficulty is in response to a double of 1♣ when you hold a flat hand with the only 4-card suit the one opened. In the first example, if partner doubles 1♣ or 1♦ bid 1♥. If he doubles 1♠ bid 2♣. In the second example, if he doubles 1♣, bid 1♦.	♠ 9 7 6 ♥ J 8 7 5 ♦ 10 6 3 ♣ 8 7 6 ♠ 9 7 6 ♥ J 8 7 ♦ 10 6 3 ♣ 8 7 6 5
A slightly stronger hand	Bid any suit held as naturally as possible, giving preference to any 4-card major which can be shown at the one-level even if a 5-card minor which must be shown at the two-level is held. Here if partner doubles 1♣ or 1♦, bid 1♥. If he doubles 1♠, bid 2♦. He will notice that the weakness response was not used though he will also notice that a stronger bid was not possible (see overleaf).	♠ 9 7 6 ♥ J 8 7 5 ♦ K 10 6 3 2 ♣ 8

Holding	Response	Examples
Stronger hand with a good biddable suit	Jump the bidding by one level, which is highly invitational but not forcing. The doubler will make every effort to reply. On this hand, if partner doubles 1♣ or 1♦, bid 2♥. If, however, he has doubled 1♠ you are not quite good enough to jump to 3♥ which might well drive the auction too high on what is, after all, only a 6-point hand, so bid 2♥.	♠ 9 7 ♥ J 10 9 8 6 4 ♦ K 10 6 ♣ 8 7
A balanced hand including a stop in the suit opened	Provided a stop in the suit opened (and doubled) is held, but only if this is sensible, bid 1NT. You should rarely make this response on a complete minimum. The alternatives of a suit bid or a negative are both available. Here if partner doubles 1♣, 1♦ or 1♥, bid 1♠. If he doubles 1♠, bid 1NT.	♠ Q J 7 4 ♥ 10 9 7 6 ♦ K 8 4 ♣ 8 7
A strong hand	On a strong hand you have a choice of a double jump expressing suit length, 2NT with a strong stop in suit doubled and other values or, particular if in doubt as to the best final denomination, a cue-bid of the suit doubled. This passes the choice of suit back to partner. Many players use this bid as forcing to suit agreement, which means that it is not	♠ K J 9 7 ♥ A J 6 4 ♦ 9 7 5 ♣ K 3

TABLE 40 *(continued)* 101

Holding	Response	Examples
	forcing to game. Here, if partner doubles 1♣ (or 1♦), bid 2♣ (or 2♦). His choice is virtually bound to be one of the majors which you can raise invitationally. With added values you would raise to game direct.	
A good holding in the suit doubled	When there has been no intervening bid to let you off the hook you are under an absolute obligation to respond to the double except on the one occasion when you wish to convert the take-out double to a penalty one by passing. This will be because you have an exceptional holding in the enemy suit which you think will defeat the doubled one-level contract for as good a score as you can get in any other contract. Sometimes this is clearly marked, sometimes difficult to judge. Here, for instance, if partner doubles 1♦ and this is passed round to you, your best, and possibly only plus score will come from defending, so pass.	♠ 9 ♥ 8 7 ♦ Q J 10 7 6 4 ♣ Q 10 8 2

TABLE 41

Action over Opponent's Take-out Double

When your partner's opening bid has been doubled by your right-hand opponent, the rules for your responding bids are quite different from those set out in Tables 5, 6 & 7. As the double in any case keeps the auction open for partner there is no need to respond without something positive to say.

The Rules	Examples
1 With a weak hand and no good suit of your own *pass* unless a bid of 1NT, showing meagre values, might obstruct opponents from discovering their own best contract. Here, if partner's opening of 1♦ has been doubled, 1NT will prevent the doubler's partner from bidding either major at the one-level. But if it is 1♠ that has been doubled no purpose is served by bidding 1NT, as any response must be given at the two-level in any case.	♠ K 8 6 ♥ Q 9 5 ♦ 10 8 7 ♣ Q 6 5 3
2 With a long suit of your own and no support for partner's suit, bid your suit at the lowest available level as a *warning* to partner. Such a bid is now a weak rescue and *not* a one-round force. Here bid 1♥ over 1♣ or 1♦ doubled. If the double is of 1♠, *pass* with your partial fit.	♠ 8 6 5 ♥ Q J 10 6 4 3 ♦ 7 ♣ 5 4 3
3 With no interest in defence but a good suit of your own and ambitions towards a game contract, make a jump bid of one level, which is encouraging but not forcing. Here, if partner's opening in any other suit is doubled, bid 2♠.	♠ K Q J 8 7 3 ♥ 7 4 3 ♦ A 7 ♣ 9 8

TABLE 41 *(continued)*

103

The Rules	*Examples*
4 Up-grade any weak suit limit-bid response your hand may hold by one level as a pre-emptive measure. Here, for example, without the intervening double you would pass partner's opening bid of 1♠. After the double, raise to 2♠, which obstructs next hand from responding at the two-level. This rule also applies to responding hands genuinely worth a raise of the opening bid to the two-level, in which case the response should be the extra jump to the three-level. On this hand you would have raised partner's opening 1♥ to 2♥ without the intervening double, so now raise to 3♥, obstructing to the greatest possible limit, and very probably making it impossible for the doubler's partner to speak at all.	♠Q853 ♥Q74 ♦763 ♣842 ♠K84 ♥A874 ♦763 ♣842
5 A responding hand on which, without the double, you would have given a genuine double-raise limit-bid to the three-level, is shown by a conventional response of 2NT. Over this opener will rebid as he would have done over a one-three raise in an uninterrupted sequence, i.e. if he would have passed a 1♥-3♥ raise, he merely converts 2NT to 3♥. If he would have gone on to 4♥, he rebids 4♥ over 2NT.	♠A106 ♥Q1075 ♦94 ♣KJ96
6 A weak responding hand with a strong trump fit and shape by way of voids or singletons can, of course, raise direct to four as a purely pre-emptive attempt, particularly at favourable vulnerability. Here, if not vulnerable against vulnerable opponents, raise partner's opening 1♥ bid, if doubled, to 4♥, which uses so much bidding space that it	♠7 ♥Q97543 ♦KJ975 ♣8

The Rules	*Examples*

may be quite impossible for the opposition to bid again.

7   A responding hand of 9 or more honour points which falls into none of the above categories is shown by a *redouble*. This does *not* promise trump support for opener though it promises at least one further bid and suggests that this may be to double the opponents' final contract. Any bid over the double, of course, removes your left-hand opponent's obligation to bid, but whether he bids or leaves action up to his partner, opener should allow the auction to come round to you again provided his hand has good prospects in defence. If opener bids again, therefore, he is showing that he does *not* wish to defend (either because weak or because of shape, or because anticipating a better score from a game or even slam contract for your side).

♠ A J 9 8
♥ 9 8
♦ K J 7
♣ Q 9 8 6

    On this last example, redouble if partner's opening 1♥ is doubled. Particularly if the opponents try a black-suit contract, you should have a lucrative penalty coming your way.

TABLE 42   105

Responding to a Take-out Double when there has been an Intervening Bid

An intervening bid of any sort over your partner's take-out double *relieves you of the obligation to respond.* Any bid you make should, therefore, be constructive. See Table 40 for what these intervening bids should mean, then judge whether or not to pass, remembering that your partner has asked you to show your best suit.

The Rules	*Examples*
Over a suit intervening bid: 1 Bid any 4-card suit, however weak the hand, if able to bid at the one-level.	♠ Q 10 7 6 ♥ K 3 ♦ 7 6 3 ♣ 10 8 7 4
2 On a somewhat better hand (4-6 points) bid any 5-card suit, even if this must be at the two-level.	1♦ – Dbl – 1♥ – 1♠
3 Always show a 5-card suit unless extremely weak and opener's partner has bid at, for you, a dangerously high level.	♠ Q 10 7 ♥ 8 6 ♦ 10 8 7 6 3 ♣ 8 7 4
4 On about 8 points upwards show any biddable suit held, jumping one level, or double responder's suit with a good holding in it.	1♣ – Dbl – 1♠ – 2♦ *but* 1♥ – Dbl – 3♥ – *NO*

The Rules	*Examples*
Over a redouble:	♠ 9 7 3
1 Pass on a worthless hand – partner has now been given another chance to bid.	♥ 9 6 4 3 ♦ J 8 2 ♣ 9 7 2
2 Bid any 4-card suit which can be shown at the one-level – this is not worthless to your partner, who has asked to be shown your best suit.	1♣ – Dbl – 1♦ – 1♥ *but* 1♣ – Dbl – 1♠ – *NO*
3 Bid any 5 or 6-card suit, even on a complete Yarborough.	♠ 9 7 3 ♥ 9 6 5 4 3 ♦ J 8 ♣ 9 7 2 1♦ – Dbl – 1♠ – 2♥

TABLE 43   107

Slam Bidding

THE BLACKWOOD CONVENTION

Either member of the partnership, without any specific holding, but when he needs to investigate first and/or second round controls in the hope of bidding a slam, may bid 4NT. This asks partner to show the number of aces held, the responses being:

No ace – 5♣   One ace – 5♦   Two aces – 5♥   Three aces – 5♠
All four aces – 5♣ (as for no aces)

A subsequent bid of 5NT asks for partner's kings on the same scale, except that 6NT is used to show all four kings.

The 4NT bid should not be used until the trump suit has been agreed, either directly or inferentially.

If an opponent intervenes over the 4NT bid the Blackwood responses are modified:

No ace – pass. One ace, five of next higher-ranking suit, etc, etc.

When the 4NT bidder finds that two aces are missing but would prefer the hand to be played in no-trumps, he cannot bid 5NT as this would be the conventional request to partner to show kings. He can, however, bid 5 of any previously unbid suit which requests partner to transfer to 5NT which he will pass.

Do not confuse the Blackwood 4NT with a quantitative raise to 4NT based on point count (see Table 23).

THE ACOL DIRECT KING CONVENTION

There are various bids which specifically deny an ace-holding (as 2♠-4♠, Table 31) or show a specific number of aces (1♠-4♣, Swiss, see Table 8). In any such situation it is pointless to waste a round of bidding to seek information already known, and a bid of 4NT is a direct request to show the number of kings held on the Blackwood scale, by-passing the request to show aces.

THE ACOL OPENING 4NT

A conventional opening bid for use on rare hands where responder's possible ace-holding is the only factor of interest to opener. The conventional responses are:

Two aces – 5NT. With the ♦A, ♥A or ♠A, five of the appropriate suit; with the ♣A – 6♣; with no ace – 5♣.

An occasion for the use of this bid would arise when it is vital for opener to know which particular ace (if two are missing) is held by his partner, an issue which might be confused by any other opening bid and a subsequent Blackwood 4NT with a 5♦ response to show one ace (which one?).

♠ K Q J 4
♥ A K Q J 10 9 7 5
♦ –
♣ A

A perfect example – 7♥ is certain if partner holds the ♠A, whilst the ♦A is so much waste paper. Open 4NT and if partner denies an ace (5♣) bid 6♥. If he bids 5♦, bid 6♥. If he bids 5♠, bid 7♥.

5NT GRAND SLAM FORCE: See Table 10.

GERBER 4♣ RESPONSE TO NO-TRUMP OPENINGS: See Table 24.

TABLE 44   109

Responses to Gambling 3NT

Bid		Examples
No bid	Responder, knowing opener's weakness in all but his running minor, should not leave 3NT unless holding some sort of guard in the other suits.	♠ Q J 10 7 4 ♥ K Q 2 ♦ A 3 2 ♣ 5 4
4♣	Not attracted by 3NT but prepared to play in either minor. Opener converts if necessary. Here opener's suit must be diamonds but 4♦ has another meaning.	♠ 9 7 6 ♥ 7 4 3 ♦ 9 5 ♣ K J 7 4 2
4♦	4♦ is an otherwise idle bid so is used to request opener to show any singleton or void he holds by a cue-bid, with a possible slam in view, for which, in this case, spade control is needed.	♠ J 6 2 ♥ A 7 ♦ A K Q 10 6 ♣ 10 7 4
4♥/4♠	Shows a good strong suit in which responder is prepared to play. Here he knows opener's suit is clubs but 4♠ should be easier than 5♣. 3NT could be disastrous.	♠ A K Q 9 7 6 4 ♥ 4 ♦ K Q 7 ♣ 8 5
4NT	Asks responder to convert to his suit at the five-level, ensuring game is reached or (optional alternative) bid a slam in his minor if his hand contains an extra trick.	♠ A K 9 8 7 ♥ A K 7 6 4 ♦ 8 ♣ 8 2
5♣	A hand on which responder wishes to be in game in opener's suit. Opener should convert if necessary. This can't be a slam hand as opener can't hold ♠A and ♦A.	♠ K Q 7 5 ♥ A K 8 3 2 ♦ K Q J 5 ♣ –

Bid		Examples
5♦	As above, but opener's suit must be diamonds, and there must be two aces missing.	♠K Q 7 5 ♥A K 8 3 2 ♦ – ♣K Q J 6
6♣/6♦	To play – a hand on which the slam should be safe provided the lead comes up to responder's hand. Here opener's suit must be diamonds and the lead up to responder's hand will protect ♠K.	♠K 6 ♥A K Q 4 2 ♦4 3 ♣A K 9 8
	If responder has bid the conventional 4♦:	
4♥	Shows a singleton or void in hearts	
4♠	Shows a singleton or void in spades	
5♣	Shows a singleton or void in *diamonds*	
5♦	Shows a singleton or void in *clubs*.	
4NT	Shows no singleton or void.	

TABLE 45   111

Directional Asking Bids

Generally known as DABS, these are bids made in the opponents' bid suit when no forcing situation exists, with a view to getting into no-trumps. Partner is requested to respond to the DAB by bidding no-trumps at the appropriate level if holding a partial stop in the opponents' bid suit, which will boost the DAB bidder's holding into at least one stop. A partial stop would be K-x, Q-x, or J-x-x. A DAB is a one-round force.

Example:

N	E	S	W
1♦	1♠	2♣	–
2♠	–	?	

♠ Q 7
♥ K J 5
♦ A K Q J 6 2
♣ Q 10

On the North hand shown below, when partner has already shown a minimum of 8 honour points, the easiest final contract is likely to be 3NT if West can supply a 'boost' to his partner's ♠Q-7. South should give preference to a response in no-trumps, bidding either 2NT or 3NT direct if his strength warrants. Failing this, he must make his best available suit rebid.

Glossary of Bridge Terms

Term	Definition
Term	*Definition*
Balanced Hand	A hand with no singleton or void. Completely balanced is 4-3-3-3 pattern. Might be 4-4-3-2 or occasionally 5-3-3-2.
Biddable Suit	A suit which, if supported by partner, will make a reasonable choice as trumps.
Business Double	See Penalty Double.
Control	The commanding position or card in a suit, enabling the holder to win a trick when the suit is led. In a trump suit contract an ace or a void is first-round control and a guarded king or a singleton is second-round control.
Convention	An artificial bid or sequence of bids carrying a meaning other than the apparent natural one.
Cue-Bid	A bid in a suit (after the trump suit has been agreed either directly or inferentially) which shows first-round control of this suit.
Delayed Game Raise	A jump bid to game in opener's suit following a simple first-round change-of-suit, by which time responder has heard opener's rebid.

Directional Asking Bid — A bid in the opponent's suit made in a non-forcing situation, or when it cannot be misunderstood, asking partner if he can supply a partial stop in this suit for a no-trump contract.

Distributional Point Count — See Table 1.

Double Jump/ Double Raise — A bid of one more level than needed for a simple raise of partner's suit (1♠-3♠).

Fit — Good mutual support in the combined hands of a partnership. Generally used to refer specifically to the trump suit, though may also include distribution.

Forcing Bid — Any bid which unconditionally demands a reply from partner. Bids may be forcing for one round only, forcing to game, or even forcing to slam.

Fourth Suit Forcing — The use of a bid in the fourth (as yet unbid) suit as responder's rebid, used as an artificial one-round force (Table 22).

Free Bid — Any bid made when the player concerned is not in the position of being *forced* to reply to his partner, as when an intervening bid has been made over the forcing bid.

Grand Slam — A contract to make all thirteen tricks.

Honours — At a suit contract, the A-K-Q-J-10 in the trump suit. At no-trumps, the four aces. These count for bonus points at rubber bridge.

Inferential Force — A bid which, though not unconditionally forcing, it is inconceivable that partner should take it upon himself to pass.

Intervening Bid	A bid made by an opponent after one player has bid and before his partner has responded.
Jump Bid	Any bid made at a higher level than the one needed to beat the previous bid, or at a higher level than necessary to show support.
Lead-directing Bid or Double	A bid, or double of an opponent's bid, made specifically to direct partner's attention to the lead required.
Limit-bid	A bid which shows the full values of the hand concerned, both upper and lower limit. Never forcing but may be highly encouraging.
Negative Response	A forced response, showing weakness or the lack of a specific holding, in reply to a forcing bid by partner.
Opening Bid	The first bid in the auction other than a pass.
Overcall	Any bid made by the player on the left of the opening bidder.
Penalty Double	A business double, intended to increase the penalty available when it is anticipated that the opponents' contract will be defeated.
Playing Trick	An expected trick for the side gaining the contract as distinct from a defensive trick.
Point Count	The scale of values used to judge the strength of any particular hand. See Table 1.
Positive Response	A response to partner's forcing bid showing positive as compared with negative values.
Pre-emptive Bid	A bid at an unnecessarily high level, made with the specific intention of depriving opponents of bidding space.

Preference Bid	A bid showing mere preference for one of partner's bid suits as compared with a supporting raise.
Prepared Bid	A bid made out of the natural sequence (possibly on a 3-card suit) in the hope of facilitating the rest of the auction.
Protective Bid	A bid made by fourth-in-hand when two passes have followed the opening bid.
Quantitative Bid	A bid showing the top limit of the hand, generally a slam invitation. Natural, limited, and non-forcing.
Raise	A bid made in support of partner's suit or no-trump bid.
Rebiddable Suit	A suit long enough and strong enough (minimum 5-cards) to be bid and rebid without support from partner.
Redouble	A bid which doubles the already augmented values of tricks or penalties for a doubled contract. Also used conventionally (e.g. following opponent's take-out double).
Responder	The partner of a player who has made a bid.
Reverse Bid	A rebid (by either opener or responder) in a suit higher in rank than the opening bid or original response.
Ruff	Use a trump to win a trick in another suit.
Sacrifice Bid	An intentional over-bid made in the hope of preventing an even worse score if opponents gain the contract. See also pre-emptive bids which come into the same category.
Shaded Bid	A bid made on somewhat less than the normal requirements.

Sign-off Bid   A rebid which indicates that the hand contains no additional values other than those already shown.

Small Slam   A contract to make twelve of the thirteen tricks.

Stop or Stopper   Any card or combination of cards which will prevent the run of that suit by opponents.

Support   See Raise.

Take-out Double   A conventional double requiring partner to show his best suit in response. Also known as Informatory Double.

Trial Bid   A bid used to investigate whether partner can assist with a weak spot.

Unbalanced Hand   A hand containing a singleton or void, or one or more predominantly long suits.

Index